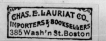

GERMANY'S MADNESS

GERMANY'S MADNESS

BY

EMIL REICH

(DOCTOR JURIS)

Author of "General History," "Foundations of Modern
Europe," "Atlas Antiquus," "Atlas of English
History," "Select Documents," "Suc-
cess Among Nations," etc.

NEW YORK
DODD, MEAD AND COMPANY
1914

VAIL-BALLOU COMPANY
BINGHAMTON AND NEW YORK

PREFACE

THE late Dr. Emil Reich, author of the trenchant volume here reprinted, was a Hungarian born, and was educated at the Universities of Prague, Budapest and Vienna, where he had ample opportunity to study the German Empire and interpret its thought and aspirations from a close and critical standpoint. Latterly he lived for many years in England, and came to identify himself entirely with Britain's welfare and interests, but he was able to claim, in a short preface, that his book was "based on a full and sympathetic study of German history and literature, both in the past and in the present."

The motive which inspired the author to put pen to paper in 1907 derived from an apprehension, only too well founded, that the British nation was by no means fully awake to the nature of German aspirations, although these were, in his opinion, fraught with menace to the peace and well-being of the British Empire. To-day, Germany, running amok in Europe, has justified his prognosis to the utmost, and Britain has been forced to face the "supreme struggle" which he foresaw.

Dr. Reich's startling exposure of the Kaiser and the governing classes of Germany did not immediately achieve its object. Indeed, the book passed almost unnoticed, for in 1907 the average Englishman still refused to believe that the Kaiser and his subjects were inspired by bitter enmity to the British Empire. Then, too, Dr. Reich's plea for the creation of a huge standing army was calculated to prejudice him in the eyes of the large mass of people whose tradition is that the nation is secure while it maintains command of the sea, and that the burden of naval expenditure is heavy enough in its drain upon the public purse, without the addition of tremendous sums to the annual army estimates. Add to this the fact that the book was published by a provincial printer, and it is possible to account for the neglect which was the portion of the first edition.

Although the book missed the public for whom it was intended, it made an impression on a few discerning minds. That astute watcher of European politics, the late King Edward, read it and was so much impressed that he recommended it to a distinguished soldier, as will be seen from the striking letter of the Bishop of Durham which appeared in the *Times* of August 17. We quote the opening paragraph:—

> "About seven years ago, I was a fellow
> guest at Trinity Lodge, Cambridge, with a
> distinguished soldier, who showed me, be-
> fore we parted, a book to which his own
> attention had been called by King Edward.
> It was *Germany's Swelled Head,* by Dr.
> Emil Reich."

No doubt the distinguished soldier was duly
impressed, and no doubt he passed the book
on to other distinguished men in both services.
Probably it is not straining the point to sug-
gest that the state of preparedness in which
Germany found us at the opening of the war
may have been not a little due to the valuable
information concerning her intentions given by
Dr. Reich.

In order to bring Dr. Reich's work up to
date, there has been added an epilogue, by another hand. This, it is believed, will make it
clear that the omens which were already above
the horizon in 1907 have, in the interval, been
reinforced by sundry dicta and data since observed by those who have kept an eye upon
European politics and on the things that were
being written, said and done in Germany.

In revising the text of Dr. Reich's original work, an attempt has been made to eliminate some of the matter that is irrelevant to the present issue; but it has been thought unnecessary to correct or qualify the author's statements as to the naval and commercial situation in the summer of 1907. These have still a certain historical significance, and in themselves form part of the case upon which Dr. Reich based his exposure of the Kaiser's dreams and the seeming apathy of the advisers of the British Government. There has been steady development in the British naval policy since 1907, and none could rejoice more than would Dr. Reich, were he still alive, in the fact that war, sudden war, has found the British navy fit and ready.

If it were necessary to justify the republication of Dr. Reich's masterly summary of German pretensions, sufficient reason would surely be found in the immediate desirability of making absolutely clear to the ordinary citizen the nature and objective of the Kaiser's policy, and the swelled-headedness of the German people which has made possible the present insane campaign.

August, 1914.

CONTENTS

PART I

Summary of the whole book, p. 1. The Kaiser—his real personality, 1–5. Potentially he is where Napoleon was in 1807, 7. Some utterances of the Kaiser, 10, 11. What he means by "German people," 11. H. S. Chamberlain's work (*Foundations, etc.*) and its enormous success in Germany. He and his school "prove" that all the great men of the past were Germans, 13–16; so was Jesus, 16, 17; and others, 17–23. Vast influence of this crazy idea, 24. Quotations from Woltmann's book proving all the great Italians of the Renascence, and the French, to have been of German origin, 24–37. How all this has created the swelled-head of the Germans, 37–38. The ignorance of Britons about Germany, 39. The Germans are upstarts, and hence intolerably conceited, 40–47. There is a "German Religion," 47. Quotations to show what the Germans are taught to think of themselves; and of the "evident" vocation of Germany, 47–67; judgments of French and Russian writers on Germany's swelled head, 67–69.

PART II

How Austria-Hungary, in her present position, contributes to the swelling of Germany's head, 72–81; and Russia, 81–82. Result: There are now only two Great Powers in Europe, Great Britain and Germany, 82. The German Navy and its constant and rapid growth, 83–101. German plans in Persia, 101–106. German prosperity, 106–109. To understand German Imperialism one must understand the real driving causes of British Imperialism, 109–113. Why Germans hate emigration, 113–118. Nor do they mean to abstain from having

ix

PART III

EPILOGUE

GERMANY'S MADNESS

PART I

The Germans are afflicted with the severest attack of swelled-headedness known to modern history.

The British are practically ignorant of this dangerous state of mind in their greatest rivals.

THESE two statements are the burden of this book. The first of them can be made out as one can prove a mathematical truth. Of the correctness of the second statement, that is, of the fact that the British, as a nation, are amazingly ignorant of the state of the German mind, the author has convinced himself in the course of very numerous lectures and conversations enabling him to learn the views of thousands and thousands of Britons of all classes, both men and women.

What, for instance, can be more astounding than the opinions commonly held in this country with regard to the Kaiser? To most Englishmen he is a kind of "impulsive young man"; a sort of reckless after-dinner talker, hasty telegraphist, jack-of-all-trades, and "commer-

1

cial traveller of the Germanic firm.'' When, in a public lecture, one speaks of him as "William the Greatest,'' the whole audience bursts into self-complacent laughter. Say at a lecture, that "the mailed fist is looming large and has to be nipped in the bud,'' and you pass for the man who has said a great political truth in a witty manner.

THE REAL KAISER

Yet there is not a grain of real judgment in all this. It is only another form of shaking hands with oneself, of patting oneself on one's back. Strange to say, this rather awkward way of stroking one's back is the most pleasing of distractions to most people talking European politics. The Kaiser is nothing less than the very reverse of what most Englishmen imagine him to be. He is, to begin with, a man of ripe, sober, and substantial judgment. On all the outstanding questions of European policy he is undoubtedly the best informed individual in existence. He knows all the great States and Nations of Europe from personal contact with them; he speaks their languages, and knows their history intimately; he is constantly kept up to the mark; and, to give just one instance, twelve experienced men of his Cabinet never stop paying the minutest attention to all military movements and military resources of the British, all the world over. The French President, or his leading ministers; the Emperor-King of Austria-Hungary; or the King of Italy, let alone the Czar of Russia, cannot, in point of real information on European politics, begin to compare with the Kaiser.

Now, knowledge of this kind *is* power. Not all knowledge is power. There is theoretic knowledge; there is newspaper knowledge; there is schoolroom wisdom; and there is the Desert of Sahara called the knowledge of the official mind. But the information possessed by the Kaiser on international politics is true and very valuable knowledge. It is in the light of this knowledge of his that we must view all his apparently rash and impulsive acts. He wires readily; he evidently likes it. But this must not induce any one to the belief that he wires first and thinks it out afterwards. His famous wire to President Krüger was, as we now know, a carefully-thought-out lightning. He wanted to embroil England in South Africa, so as to win time for his naval preparations. Prussian policy always has been what soldiers call *ricochet* shooting: one aims at A, but shoots at B.

The Kaiser clearly and definitely knows what he is about. In France, the statesmen are crippled by the false position of a defeated nation, chafing unspeakably under her defeat, not yet able to wash out the blot; in Austria-Hungary, the unending conflicts of the various nationalities paralyse all consistent and great statesmanship; in Italy, the Pontiff saps the King; Russia is too busy at home to think of Europe. In Germany alone, of all Continental great Powers, is there a European policy clearly grasped and energetically carried out. In Germany alone, of all Continental countries, is there a ruler, young, strong, well-informed, and pursuing a definite, well-founded, and well-organised international policy. To speak of such a ruler as most Britons do, is nothing short of absurd; absurd, from the British standpoint, we submit. The point is not to bandy jokes at this or that failing of good taste in the Kaiser; the point is to know what he is after, and if he can realise his plans. The point is to see his real proportions; to do, by him, what most people do with themselves: to take him seriously.

Really, the chief reason why so many people

fail to appreciate the Kaiser aright, is his constant making of speeches. Britons dislike words; more especially spoken words. The man who talks much is here in this country not held to be a man of power. His words, his speeches discredit him. However that may be in Great Britain, on the Continent people constantly talk. Although the average Briton may deem it almost incredible, it is a fact that people on the Continent have long conversations. They *do* listen to good speeches with deference; and men in power are expected to deliver fine speeches. The Kaiser is a born orator. He speaks naturally very well, and even the style of his addresses, delivered on the spur of the moment, is quite remarkable. Whether he delivers a sermon on board ship, as he has frequently done; or whether he addresses students at Bonn University, a regiment, labourers, scientific congresses, or diplomatists; he invariably succeeds in giving point and life and fine shape to his ideas. On the Continent this is a serious power. To underrate it, to judge it from the British standpoint, is not only absurd, but also quite beyond the point. A man who can talk as well as the Kaiser would be a prominent man in Germany under all conditions; but that such great oratory should be the gift of a person who happens to be the German Emperor, that is a fact of far-reaching importance with a nation with whom Authority and high-class oratory have an enormous influence.

THE KEYNOTE OF HIS POLICY

We shall soon see what constitutes the evident and only aim of the Kaiser. His well-known utterance, to the effect that the future of the Germans lies on the water, is the keynote of all his policy. The past of the Germans evidently "lay on beer," to imitate the Kaiser's phraseology; the future, bowing to modern teetotalism, lies on water. How many good or poor jokes can be made on that utterance! How many have been made! Yet, the point of all points is to find out whether in that teetotalising of German policy, the Kaiser has or has not struck the true keynote on which his nation will act. We unhesitatingly say, he *has* struck it. There is no other keynote to the future of Germany.

Under these conditions, the words and acts of the Kaiser must be taken very seriously indeed. His personal intervention in nearly all important questions of European politics indicates a master will and an intellect fully conscious of Germany's vast possibilities. English papers have talked of his diplomatic raid on Morocco as of a Lohengrin venture. But the Kaiser's ship carrying him to the coast of the Shereefian Empire was not a swan, and he is no Lohengrin. In fact, the shortest consideration of the facts of the present international policy in Europe will show to any one not fatally blinded by prejudice or conceit, that the Kaiser is potentially where Napoleon the Great was, exactly one hundred years ago. In 1807, in summer, Napoleon was at the height of his power. He had, in open battle, as well as in the council-room, beaten all the Great Powers of the Continent. All the German rulers, and first of all, the "Roman Emperor of the Germanic Empire," or the Austrian ruler, were utterly defeated by him. So were the Princes and Republics of Italy; and last, not least, the King of Prussia and the Czar of Russia, whom Napoleon had worsted both at Austerlitz (1805) and Friedland (1807). On the Continent, then, there was, in 1807, no Power that could seriously think of thwarting Napoleon, whether alone or allied with one or two other Powers.

Such was the state of the Continent exactly one hundred years ago. We here submit, that potentially, at any rate, the state of the Continent is at present (1907) quite the same sort of a "one man's show," as it was in 1807.

The Germans themselves look upon France as a nation that has practically given up the political game altogether. The French, says one of Germany's most popular and influential thinkers, are evidently retiring into an idyllic life, and have abandoned all hopes of playing a great *rôle* in the councils of Europe (Eduard von Hartmann). In other and more recent articles, the French are styled by the Germans, "the bankers of Europe." Thus does Germany construe the silence of France during these thirty-six years.

Austria-Hungary, and Russia, both of them beaten States, are seriously troubled by internal dissensions, and the Germans are practically free from the danger of being suddenly attacked by one or two of their Continental neighbours; just as was Napoleon in 1807. They have signally defeated both Austria and France, their most dangerous neighbours. As to Russia, Germany has had no war with a Czar since 1762; and there is, at present, no reason to think that Russia will attack Germany.

From this it follows with irrefutable cer-

tainty, that Germany in 1907 is in a position
even stronger than that of Napoleon in 1808.
For, Napoleon had in that year commenced his
unending and most troublesome wars with the
Spanish; and, although his Generals defeated
the Spanish armies time after time, he could
not secure the peaceful possession of the Peninsula. Nor was he safe with Austria. In 1809
he had to wage a new and very complicated
campaign against Austria; and when in 1812 he
invaded Russia, his Spanish wars were still
going on, all over Spain and Portugal. Now,
the Germans see themselves at present in a far
more favourable condition. They have little
to fear from France, Spain, Austria, or Italy.
Their hands are free. The Kaiser can, without
fear of unexpected surprises, concentrate his
forces upon England or Russia, or any other
objective. No other monarch on the Continent
can claim a similar position of absolute freedom of action.

Can it, under these circumstances, astound
any one that the Kaiser has a full consciousness
of his unprecedented possibilities? In speeches
without number he has given expression to his
pride and strength and aggressiveness. In a
speech delivered at the completion of a fort on

the Western frontier of Germany, he said: "I christen thee Fort Haeseler. Thou wilt be called upon to defend the conquests of Germany upon her Western foes." (March 1, 1900.) On another occasion he said:—

"I have no fear for the future, I am convinced that my plan will succeed. I have within me the indomitable purpose to walk with a firm step, in despite of every resistance, in the path that I have once recognised to be the right one."

"If one wishes to settle something in this world, the pen is only powerful so long as it is backed by the power of the sword."

Again, when laying the foundation stone of the Royal Museum at Saalburg (October 4, 1900) after consecrating the building to the future of the German Fatherland:—

"May it in times to come, by the unified co-operation of princes and peoples, of their armies and their citizens, become as powerful, and as firmly united, as wonderful as the universal Roman Empire, so that one day it may be possible to say, as formerly, *"Civis Romanus sum,"* i. e., "I am a *German citizen.*"

On October 28, 1900, when celebrating Moltke's birthday, he emitted a wish that, "the

Staff might lead Germany on to further victories,'' and again: ''My utmost wish is to re-
move whatever divides the great German people.''

THE PAN-GERMAN IDEA

For the full understanding of these latter
words, the non-German reader must be warned
not to take the term ''German people'' lightly.
By ''German,'' the Germans understand at
present practically all the nations worth talking
about. ''German'' no longer means the people
between the Rhine and the Vistula; that is, the
nation that talks German, drinks beer, and
makes music in the streets, in beer-gardens, and
in concert-halls; the nation of ''poets and
thinkers'' as the elder Lord Lytton used to call
them. By ''German'' is now understood the
vast ocean of peoples who talk a Teutonic language, and who, if they do not talk a Teutonic
idiom, ought in common decency to talk one.
The Swedes, Norwegians, Danes, Dutch; the
English, the Belgians, the Swiss; the Austrians,
the Russian Kurlanders, Lithuanians; the numerous tribes in Hungary talking German dialects; all these people are, so runs the gospel of
modern German scholars, really Germans.

Lest the reader should believe that the contemporary Germans are so modest as to claim only Sweden, Norway, Holland, Belgium, Switzerland, Hungary, Western Russia, and the little islands called British, the author hastens to add that the most influential writers in the Fatherland teach the Germans the following amusing lesson: The Slavs too, that is, the Russians, Poles, Bohemians, Servians, Croatians, etc., are, originally, all Germans.

Perhaps the reader would like to see a quotation or two about this remarkable discovery. While most of us have, thanks to the wisdom of Parliament, accustomed ourselves to learn that most material things have been "made in Germany"; many people are still innocently believing, that some nations, at any rate, were not made in the Fatherland. The error is profound. All the great nations are, we now hear from hundreds of University chairs, from thousands of journalistic pulpits, really German, and ought therefore to be submerged in One Universal Germany.

Amongst the various "world-famous" men trumpeting about this doctrine of Pan-Germanism, or *Alldeutschland;* that is, that all historic nations, in order to reach their final bliss, must and will be minced up into the Great German Universal Sausage. This doctrine, dished up to the German nation by some of their most serious writers and scholars of Berlin, Munich, Strassburg, or Leipsic, is taught, more particularly by a man who, by the irony of fate, goes by the name of Chamberlain; Houston Stewart Chamberlain. The book in which he advances his startling propositions is entitled *The Foundations of the XIXth Century,* and it has had a most marvellous success with the Germans. Although heavy, both in bulk and price, it sold in many, many thousands of copies, and is, by the majority of the Germans, considered to be a higher revelation of truth unfathomable. Rich men have bought up thousands of copies of this grostesque and absurd work, distributing them, free of charge, to hundreds of Public Libraries. The Kaiser publicly and warmly approved of it. It has given rise to quite a literature on, for, or against it; and Chamberlain is now one of the most popular and influential writers in Germany.

The secret of Chamberlain's very great success in Germany is not far to seek. With an air of scientific argument he proves to his own, and to German satisfaction, that all history spells "German," and that all future developments of the world will be "Made in Germany." The Germans are indeed, Chamberlain teaches, *the* elect people. It is mere frivolity to think that the Jews are the elect ones. By no means; the Germans are the ones, the unique, the only, the overmen, the chosen people. (That is probably the principal reason why they so hate the Jews. It is professional envy. Clearly, the Germans, not the Hebrews, are the Jews, the chosen people.) It is none of their fault. Many of them, being of a modest turn, regret being so immensely superior to other tribes. But they cannot help it. It is in them; Nature has been so kind to them. They lift their arms; and all resistance vanishes into the fourth dimension. They look at any thing, event, or riddle, and, piercing it through and through with the darts of their unfailing intellect, they solve, explain, or reconstruct it. Their stomach is strong; they can and will absorb all the mountains, meadows, rivers, seas; and their digestion will not suffer in the least.

This, then, is the gospel according to Mr. Houston Stewart Chamberlain. He says:—

"By Germans, I mean the various populations of Northern Europe who appear in history as Kelts, Germans, Slavs, and from whom, mostly in inextricable confusion, the peoples of modern Europe are sprung. That they came originally from a single family is certain, but the German, in the narrower Tacitean sense, has kept himself so pre-eminent among his kinsmen intellectually, morally, and physically, that we are justified in applying his name to the whole family. The German is the soul of our culture. The Europe of to-day, spread far over the globe, exhibits the brilliant result of an infinitely varied ramification. What binds us into one is the Germanic blood. . . . Only Germans sit on European thrones. What has happened is only *prolegomena*. . . . True history begins from the moment when the German, with mighty hand, seizes the inheritance of antiquity.''

It would be waste of time to quote here one hundredth of the passages in which that Teuton Chamberlain shows and "proves," that in the Germans, and in them alone, there is that mysterious something-or-other, that has enabled men of German blood to do the great things of the past. Of course, all the great men of the past were, when you scrutinise them more closely, nothing but Germans. So was, for instance, Dante, whose face, Chamberlain says, is "characteristically German." So was, one need scarcely insist, St. Francis of Assisi; and Pascal, whom some people are still foolish enough to consider one of the greatest of Frenchmen, was, the redoubtable Chamberlain says, nothing more nor less than a German. Did he not oppose the Jesuits?

After these master-strokes of critical analysis, no one, we hope, will feel inordinately moved by reading what Chamberlain has to say about Jesus. One is, of course, nowadays, quite used to hearing all sorts of remarks on the great personalities of the Bible. Moses has long been reduced to an emigration-agent, or to the modest predecessor of Messrs. Thomas Cook and Son. David, otherwise quite a nice young man, has long been shown up as a plagiarist, who took, it is true, his best inspirations from the hacks of the "British Museum" in Jerusalem, four hundred years after his death. All this is well known. We are likewise quite prepared to Campbellize the central figure of Christianity into a fairly successful cardboard model of a goody-goody man. But how immeasurably greater than all this is Chamberlain! He has it, at first hand, that Jesus was

no Jew at all. He has no doubt about it. He
says with the simplicity so characteristic of
Prussian thought:—

"Whoever maintains that Christ was a Jew
is either ignorant or dishonest: ignorant if he
confuses religion and race, dishonest if he
knows the history of Galilee. ، . . The probability that Christ was not a Jew, that He had
not a drop of pure Jewish blood in His veins,
is so great that it is almost a certainty. To
what race did He then belong? To that there
is no answer. . . ."

After which, Chamberlain indulges in conjectures. Perhaps, he says, Jesus was an As-
syrian colonist. On further consideration, he
finds that Assyria won't do. He then turns
westward, and opines that Jesus was probably
a Greek. This inability of Mr. Chamberlain
to find the obvious, is rather strange. Some
men of genius are like that. Although there
can, seriously speaking, be no doubt whatever
to what great nation Jesus did belong, Chamberlain, the apostle of that great nation, failed
to see it. How strange! How wonderfully in-
tricate are the paths of thy wanderings, oh
Truth!

But Germany is greater even than Mr. H. S.

Chamberlain. In due time, she went into trav-
ail and gave birth to the man who saw what
Mr. Chamberlain could not see. We mean, of
course, the obvious fact, the manifest truth, that
Jesus—was a German. The kind reader is
asked to study a ponderous volume by J. L.
Reimer, entitled "A Pan-German Germany"
(*Ein Pangermanisches Deutschland*, 1905) on
pages 232, 233. There he will find arguments
expressed in the best University slang of Berlin, and submitted with becoming seriousness,
to the effect that, if Jesus was not of German
origin, He was a fraud. Nobody can sincerely
say He was a fraud. *Ergo*, He was a German.
Or was He not blond? Had He not blue eyes,
and that roseate skin so clearly indicative of
German complexion? If this is not convincing
(and of course there are men so obdurate as not
to be convinced by any argument of that kind)
then one has only to analyse the name of Jesus.
The first syllable, *Jes*, is clearly an altered
Ger—, the letter *r* being frequently treated as
a vowel, and so dropped altogether, or changed
into *s*. The second syllable *-us*, is only the
Latin ending for males, hence equal to the German (or English) *man*. Can anything be more
evident?

It is thus quite beyond any reasonable doubt, say the German thinkers, that all Northern, North-Western, Central, Eastern, and South-Eastern nations are really Germans. When, therefore, the Kaiser speaks of Greater Germany, of the Germans in general, he, in all sincerity, means two-thirds of Europe. He means that the German Empire of the near future will, and by right of Race ought to, comprise two-thirds of Europe.

This, we are convinced, will appear to most British readers too childish an idea to be worth serious consideration. The average man in England will say to himself: "Even granted that a few writers in Germany do entertain such extravagant ideas, surely one cannot admit that the bulk of the Germans accept them as serious principles of German politics. In all countries there have been single eccentrics who absurdly overrated the significance and importance of their nation. Scotsmen have laboriously proved that Adam was a Scot. Some Englishmen have written heavy books on the English being the 'lost ten tribes.' Americans, if we are to believe some of their writers, nearly all come from Oliver Cromwell; and, as Thackeray used to say, one cannot wonder that The

Conqueror won the battle of Hastings, since so
many ancestors 'came over with the Conqueror.' "

There is much common sense in all this.   Single eccentrics do not prove very much as to the
state of mind of the majority of a people.
Some years ago the author met at the British
Museum a countryman of his, a Hungarian, who
spent all his time and wasted all his efforts
on a book in which he undertook to prove that
all the great leaders of mankind were Hungarians.   The only difference with regard to such
solitary "cranks" is this—nobody cares for
what they say or write.   Their works are believed in only by a few fellow-invalids, and en-
joyed by knowing lovers of odd books.   But,
in the case of Germany, as she has recently developed, the state of affairs is essentially and
completely different.

That which, in other countries, never rises beyond a mere oddity is, in contemporary Germany, a vast wave of national thought.   In the
Fatherland, as has long been remarked by many
an observing traveller or scholar, the writers,
teachers, journalists, and scholars of the day
have an infinitely greater influence on the people, than similar brain-workers ever wield in

England. German political unity was really set
in motion by German thought, that is, by the incredible influence of German professors, poets,
and writers. Once these bookmen take up an
idea, be it ever so nebulous, it is sure to fall,
in due time, as fertilising rain upon the rough
soil of Germany.

The reader is therefore asked never to forget that, no matter how laughable and childish
those Pan-German ideas may be, they are at the
same time most serious, on account of the effect
they have had on the Germans. In this world
there is no greater power than effect. To laugh
at a thing because it is laughable is, in political
matters, most unsound. Once already, in the
sixteenth century, a German undertook something that moved the then Pope to peals of
laughter. It appeared to Pope Leo X. too
ludicrous for words that Luther, a poor and
helpless Austin monk and professor in Germany, wanted to upset the Papal power. Yet
that helpless German did upset very much of
the Papal power. The Pope's power seemed
then as great, if not very much greater, than is
the power of the British navy to-day.

If, then, we are now going to tell the reader
more of the boundlessly fatuous ideas enter-

tained by the Germans with regard to the power, destiny, and "evident vocation" of their Race, we do so firstly, because we should like to warn him of the very great danger implied in beliefs of that kind shared by practically all the sixty million Germans; secondly, and only as a minor motive, because we want him to enjoy thoroughly the grim humour of the thing.

ALL GREAT MEN HAVE BEEN GERMANS!

We have seen that the Kaiser and the most popular writers in Germany have rapidly come to the conclusion that all the great men of the past, from Jesus downwards, were either pure or mixed Germans. But, so far, we have heard this statement only as a vague opinion. Now we are going to see how elaborately this statement has been proved in various works written by German scholars.

The underlying contention of the whole matter is, of course, very transparent. The Germans who boldly say that the twentieth century is theirs, just as the sixteenth belonged to the Spanish, the seventeenth to the French, and the eighteenth to the English, the Germans, we say, want to go one better than all the nations. For, while the Spanish or English were satisfied to

call one century theirs, the Germans want to
show, not only that the twentieth century will
be theirs, but that as a matter of fact all the
preceding centuries were, properly considered,
also theirs.

Such views would not appeal very strongly
to the English, who as a rule, do not trouble
themselves very much about former centuries.
But, in Germany, thanks to the great attention
paid to the teaching of history in all the public
schools, every schoolboy knows the names of
Italy, France, or Spain. Everybody there
knows something about Dante, Raphael,
Michelangelo Buonarotti, Leonardo da Vinci,
Machiavelli; or such Frenchmen as Rabelais,
Montaigne, Pascal, Descartes. He has, when
young, been taught to consider these men as the
glories of humanity. When, now, a learned
German proves to him, in an elaborate book,
that all these summits were only peaks of the
German Alps, the effect upon that German is
immense. His pride in his nationality is increased and intensified to an extraordinary degree. He cannot help thinking that German
blood, German ideas, German influence, and, in
short, everything German has by nature something utterly superior to anything non-German.

The whole perspective of life is changed within him. He alters his former bearings; he takes a new view of the world; that is, he gets what the Germans call a world-view, or *Weltanschauung* of a new type.

To underrate this sort of thing, to speak lightly of such a wholesale change in the mentality of the nation which, amongst advanced peoples in Europe, is the most populous, would be too futile for words. On the contrary, we have to weigh it very carefully; we must take it into close consideration. It is out of such vague but persistent feelings that a nation forges its most formidable weapons of aggressiveness.

It is for this reason that we are here going to give a few extracts from the works of Ludwig Woltmann, who, in two books published recently, tells the Germans that most of the immortals of Italy and France were, properly speaking, of German blood. The British reader may not, and we trust will not, agree with the opinions of Mr. Woltmann. This, however, is not the point at all. The real interest is in the fact that Woltmann's views have been taken by the Germans very seriously indeed, that they have been, and are being discussed in the gravest of German historical and ethnological reviews, and that their effect upon the average German is nothing short of extraordinary. In other words, the late Woltmann may be, and we have no doubt, *is* hopelessly wrong; but the effect of his works on the most responsible of German writers and readers is very considerable.

His chief instrument in proving that the great men of the Italian Renascence, or the wonderful painters, sculptors, thinkers, and poets of fifteenth and sixteenth century Italy, were all Germans, is thus constructed. Woltmann, together with a great number of English and Continental anthropologists, takes it for granted, that there are in Europe a number of separate Races. More especially, there is the Northern or Germanic Race, with a long head (*dolichocephalic*), blond hair, and blue eyes; and the Mediterranean Race, with a short and round head, and swarthy complexion. Whenever he finds that an Italian is reported as having been of a long-headed, blond, and blue-eyed appearance, he has little doubt that the mother of that Italian had, if secretly, preferred the embraces of some doughty German. And if one considers that the Germans have at all times been the roving mercenaries, lackeys,

clerks, and waiters of all Europe, it is not impossible to assume that wherever Mr. Woltmann needs a German substitute for the more
legitimate work of paternity, he can freely
draw upon some one German lackey or butler
or waiter for the emergency.

In order to fortify his surreptitious fathers
in their claims to glory, Woltmann makes free
use of that beautiful method of German philo-
logians, by means of which one can conveniently
prove what one pleases. Thus, it is not quite
evident to the untutored mind of the ordinary
mortal how Mr. Cecil Rhodes can be said to be
of the family of the late President Krüger.
But for a German philologian this apparently
impossible problem does not offer serious difficulties. Rhodes is named—who can doubt it?
—after the famous island in the Eastern Mediterranean, of which the Greek proverb used to
say: "Here is Rhodes—jump here!" meaning,
that any man boasting of his being able to jump
anything, was asked at Rhodes to jump the
width of the enormous harbour of the capital
of that island. That clearly proves that Cecil
Rhodes was boastful. So was, some people say,
the late President Krüger. Accordingly, both
were of the same family. To disguise that,

Cecil Rhodes, who was so fond of Greek and
Roman antiquities as to have nearly all the
Greek and Latin classics specially translated
for his use, chose a classical name suggestive
of a colossus, the colossus of Rhodes. Can any-
thing be simpler? In very much the same way,
Herr Woltmann shows that most of the great
Renascence men of Italy were Germans.

The reader is asked to read the following extracts from Woltmann's *Die Germanen und die
Renaissance in Italien* (1905) with great attention.

Again and again we beg to remind the reader
that the evident absurdity of Woltmann's views
is not the point at all. We deal here with the
mental state of a whole nation. A people like
the modern Germans, who can take such views
in dead earnestness, are either hopelessly decadent, or dangerously excited, overweeningly
conceited, and perilously swelled-headed. Now,
it is an absolute fact that Woltmann's views
have been taken very seriously indeed.

One of the oldest, most respectable *Profes-
soren-Blatt,* or reviews, written mostly by and
for German University Professors, the *Beilage*
(Supplement) to the *Münchener Allgemeine
Zeitung,* and other reviews (especially the

Literarisches Centralblatt) equally serious,
have reported on Woltmann's book, with a
gravity and an interest generally devoted to
first-class scientific works only. In reading the
following extracts, the British citizen must
therefore be aware of the fact that he is reading
an absurd opinion shared by thousands of
highly instructed and influential Germans. We
leave it to our readers to appreciate the political dangerousness of such opinions.

Woltmann takes one great Renascence Italian after the other, and comes to the conclusion that they were all Germans. He says:

"BENVENUTO CELLINI (1500-71).—His portrait by Vasari is in the Palazzo Vecchio in the
picture representing Cosimo in the circle of the
artists of his time: a head-piece between Cosimo and Tribolo seated at his left. The hair
on his head is brown and slightly disposed in
locks, the beard blond, inclining to reddish. To
judge from the photograph, the eyes are light
in colour, presumably blue, as blue eyes alone
are wont to give in photography so light a re-
flex." (p. 75.)[1]

"MICHELANGELO BUONAROTTI (1475-1564).—

---

[1] Surely the painting itself might have been seen by this
erudite German.—ED.

(=Bernhard) ancestor of the family, lived in Florence about 1210. He had two sons, Berlinghieri and Buonarrota, the former of whom had likewise a son, Buonarrota. By this name, recurring frequently in later generations, the family came to be called. It is a German name, compounded of Bona (=Bohn [probably the ancestors of the publishers, Messrs. Bell and Son,] Bonne) and Hrodo, Roto (=Rohde, Rothe), Bona and Rotto are cited as Lombard names. Buonarotti is perhaps the old Lombard Beonrad, corresponding to the word Bonroth. Corresponding names are Mackrodt, Osterroth, Leonard. According to Condivi the Buonarroti spring from the family of the Counts of Canossa, a noble Lombard gens in the territory of Reggio, related to the Emperor Henry II. In point of fact the Counts of Canossa always looked on the artist as a relation. Of Michelangelo's bodily presence we have precise and essentially accordant descriptions by Vasari and Condivi. In his *Life of M.B.* A. Condivi writes: 'Michelangelo is of well-built body, sinewy and bony rather than fleshy and fat; sound, more than anything else, both by nature, by bodily exercise and by abstinence, though as a child he was weakly and subject to fits. In his face he has always been well-coloured. Of medium stature, he is broad shouldered, but in the rest of his body weak rather than robust. The temples strongly project, more than the ears. His nose has a somewhat crushed appearance, not by nature, but from the stroke of a fist he received in his youth on the cartilage of the nose. The brow in profile projects beyond the nose. The eyebrows have a scanty fringe of hair. The eyes might be called small rather than large, of the colour of horn, but variable with "flecks" of yellow and blue. Hair and beard are black. These particulars are confirmed by the portraits. First and foremost take the portrait by Bugiardini in Museo Buonarroti. Here comes to view the "flecked" appearance of the iris, especially in the right eye. The left may be described as almost wholly blue. The lateral projection of the skull over the ears is to be explained by an abnormal growth of bone. Michel appears to have been rachitic and hydrocephalus, which may be connected with the fits of his youth. From the remark that his face was highly coloured, it may be concluded that his cheeks were of fresh, ruddy hue. In the Museo Civico, at Pavia, is a fresco likeness by an unknown hand, in which this fresh red is distinctly recognisable on the face. Taking all these bodily characteristics into consideration, it must be said from an anthropological point of view that though originally of German family, he was a hybrid between the North and West brunette race.' " (pp. 73-4.)

"LORENZO GHIBERTI (1378-1455).—The name of the Ghiberti, who are first mentioned in 1260 among the Guelf families in Florence, is derived from Old High German Wiberto Guiberto, New High German Wilbert. As Vasari reports in *Life of L.G.,* he set his likeness in the bronze of the Baptistery in Florence. In his work Vasari presents a profile likeness evidently drawn after this bronze head. I have more minutely studied the anthropological characteristics of this head on a gypsum cast. The skull is very long and small, index about 73, therefore pronouncedly dolichocephalic. The face, too, is long and small, the nose lightly curved, the hair disposed in locks, though nothing is reported as to the colour of the hair and eyes, yet, on the ground of the family name and the build of head and face, we may with great certainty assume that he was descended from the Germans." (pp. 69-70.)

"GIOVANNI BELLINI (1426-1507) has left two likenesses by himself; one in the Uffizi, the other in the Conservatoire Palace in Rome. Both show German features of face, light straw yellow hair and blue eyes. Bellini is from Old High German Belo, Bella, Bellin." (p. 80.)

"LEONARDO DA VINCI (1452-1517) or, as he called himself, Leonardo Vinci, came of a noble family, the earliest extant document about whom, dated 1339, is signed by a Florentine notary. He was born in an old Castle to the N. of Empoli, of which a tower and some walls still remain. The Castle, in olden time 'Casserodi Vinci,' is evidently named after a German Knight Vinco (= Winke, Vincke). In the neighbourhood are several castles and villages with old German names, such as Cerreto Guidi, Lamporrechio (= Lamprecht) and Tizzana (Tizzo = Tietz). Some mile and a half (halbe Stunde) NE. of Vinci, on the slope of Monte Albano, lies a 'Luogo d'Anchiano,' where a Castle is said to have formerly stood, the name of which is derived from the old German Ango (= Anke, Enke). Here the family Vinci had a country house, in which was born Leonardo, in the midst of a district once peopled by Germans. In the valleys and on the slopes of

Monte Albano, at a distance from the great
highway, you still find among the peasantry
many blond and blue-eyed men, in all likelihood
the remains of the Gothic tribe. Out of this
soil sprang the otherwise unknown Caterina,
mother of Leonardo, a lady, '*que era di bon
sangue*,' of a robust and sound stamp of humanity. Like his nephew Pieroda Vinci, a
sculptor, Leonardo was tall and strong in bodily
make, the hair of his head and his beard hang-
ing down to the middle of his chest. The likeness of himself in red chalk in the Pinacothec
at Turin shows the head of a greybeard, with
small, high-arched brow, small face, and
slightly aquiline nose. A profile likeness in
Windsor Library presents a skull of great
measure lengthwise. In the 'self-likenesses' in
the Uffizi, is a portrait of Leonardo, though not
possibly by Leonardo himself, and it may be
assumed to have been taken from life. It
shows him with blond hair on head, blond beard,
and blue eyes. Leonardo's blond complexion
is not reported in so many words by his biog-
raphers, but the constantly extolled beauty of
his hair almost implies it, seeing that for the
Italian, and especially of the Renaissance,
blond hair was the characteristic of physical

beauty. A figure in 'The Three Archangels and Tobias'—by Verrochio, according to the prevailing view—presents the picture of a slim and tall-grown youth, with large blue eyes, yellow hair, finely shaped and expressive features, which one may conjecture to be the portrait of Leonardo. Altogether, from biographical and iconographic sources, Leonardo's anthropological features may be summed up as follows: Tall and strong figure; long and small skull; face of like conformation, with lightly curved nose, light complexion, large blue eyes; blond hair of head curled in ringlets; blond beard. If any among the great Italians, Leonardo was a pure and unmixed scion of the German race." (pp. 83-6.)

"RAFFAEL SANTI (1483-1520).—As shown by Passavant, there lived in Colbordolo, Raffael's father's birthplace, about the first half of the fourteenth century a certain Sante, giving the family name of Sante or Santi to his descendants. The name of the Castle Colbordolo is of old German origin, analogous to Heribord, Heltiport, and similar names. Like its derivatives Santini, Santoni, Santi is equally a German name, corresponding to Sandt in New High German. Raffael's mother, Magia

Ciarla, was the daughter of a merchant in Urbino. According to Muratori, Ciarla is said to be derived from Charles and to have been brought to Italy by the Franks. In this case it would be equivalent to the old German Carla. Nothing certain is known of the bodily presence of Raffael's father, Giovanni. In the *case di Raffaelo* in Urbino, however, is a fresco likeness, let into the wall, from Giovanni's hand, presenting Frau Magia and Raffael as Madonna with the Bambino. It is remarkable how scanty are the notices left by his contemporaries regarding Raffael's exterior. Raffael's likeness of himself in the Uffizi shows us the painter at the age of twenty-three. This picture has, however, been several times painted over, and only mouth and nose remain intact. In this portrait we find Raffael with a nobly shaped and small face, soft grey eyes, with a slight inclination to brownish, and dark blond hair shading into reddish.

"In the Berlin Museum is an altar piece of Giovanni Santi, representing Mary and the Child Jesus, which has always been taken to be the image of Raffael and his mother. Both have light blond hair. The child has blue eyes, whereas the mother has grey eyes, dashed with a bluish and brownish glimmer. In the fresco likeness at Urbino above-mentioned, both have light blond hair. The child's eyes are unfortunately closed, the mother's are of a mixed grey. There is further, a likeness of Raffael in his sixteenth year, ascribed to his father, a good copy of which is in the Hanover Museum. Here Raffael has yellow blond hair and dark grey eyes. In the Libreria of Siena Cathedral, Raffael and his teacher Pinturicchio are, in *Catherine's Canonization,* presented, full figure, as taper bearers. Both have blond hair and rosy-white skin. Whereas, however, Pinturicchio shows eyes of distinct blue, corresponding to those of his self-portrait in Spello, Raffael has grey-yellow eyes. To this likeness of Raffael by Pinturicchio, then his teacher, must be attached the greatest importance in forming a judgment of his physical type. Of the identity there can be no doubt. Here more particularly is the so characteristic dropping of the upper eyelid. Altogether it may with great certainty be concluded that in his youth Raffael had light blond hair and bluish eyes, but with advancing age hair and eyes assumed a somewhat darker shading.

"Raffael's skeleton, found in the Pantheon,

was five feet two inches, Parisian measure =
167·5 cm. long. The skull was small.

"G. K. Nagler, too, in his *Raffael als
Mensch und Künstler* writes: 'His features
were of regular beauty, the eye clear and pure,
the mirror of a beautiful soul; the form of the
head was oval, and the hair blond till with the
progress of the years it inclined slightly to
brownish.' " (pp. 89-91.)

The British reader of the preceding extracts
will probably think that in such stuff and twad-
dle there is not much to frighten serious men.
Nor is there. We do not mean to assert
that the stuff itself, or, in other words, that
Herr Woltmann's misplaced erudition, has, by
itself, any value whatever. The great men of
the Italian Renascence were no more German
in mind or body than they were Yankees. But
what cannot be taken too seriously, we contend,
is the *effect* of such stuff on the mind of the
German nation. The stuff is wretched enough,
but its effect is a most important matter.

RESULTANT SWELLED-HEADEDNESS

One can readily understand that the British,
themselves, calm in their strength, are inclined
to treat such vagaries as strong men generally

treat the extravagances of boys. But one cannot quite understand that the British, on learning that these vagaries of a great number of German writers have fairly dazed the German people, still continue to smile with tranquillity. This, it would appear to us, is in the highest degree impolitic. The actions of a nation like the Germans are, in the first place, influenced by their state of mind; and, given that that state of mind in Germany is now one bordering on absolute *megalomania,* or the most morbid form of self-conceit and swelled-headedness, it is safe to conclude that their actions, too, will soon assume forms of the most daring self-assertiveness and aggression.

In this country, Germany and the Germans are practically as unknown and as poorly understood as if they lived somewhere in Central Asia, and not within eight hours' sailing from England. Their literature is so little known that more than once the author was asked by Englishmen whether the Germans had three or four writers of note. The following story is absolutely true, if intensely humorous. A rich city merchant invited to one of his receptions a number of literary people. The conversation for a time touched upon German literature, and amongst other names that of Goethe was frequently mentioned. The host had never heard that name before. Rather annoyed by the constant recurrence of that name, he asked one of his literary guests who Goethe was. He received the answer that Goethe was one of the great German poets. Thereupon the city merchant indignantly exclaimed: "Of course, we know him, but we call him over here 'Schiller' "!

What, indeed, does the average Briton know of the vast wave of Imperialism that has flooded the hearts and the minds of the Germans? Does he ever read the *Alldeutsche Blätter,* the organ of the Pan-Germanists? [2] Does he study the *Deutsche Erde,* a geographical review devoted to Pan-German interests? Has he ever heard of the periodicals and books treating of the "necessary," "inevitable," and "providential" spread of the German Empire over Europe and the globe? Has he ever attempted to appreciate aright the effect of this constant and unremitting excitement of imperialist fever that has, these twenty-five years, seized the Germans? It never enters his mind to think of it, to pay the slightest attention to

[2] Even the British Museum Library has no copy of it.

it. Occasionally, it is true, the Briton is roused to anger or indignation by an utterance or act of the Kaiser or his Chancellor. However, influential as these two dignitaries may be, they are not the most effective of the Imperialists in Germany. The most effective are those German authors who, like Professor Treitschke, Herr Woltmann, Mr. H. S. Chamberlain, Herr Reimer, Herr Hasse, Count Ernst Reventlow, and a host of others, instil the poison of *megalomania* into the Germans in the one manner in which the Germans will take it in the largest doses.

GERMANY IS AN UPSTART

Perhaps the following consideration will help the reader to see the matter in its true proportions. The most ignorant is aware of the fact that Germany is an upstart; that her existence as a Great Power is, so to speak, of yesterday. As to Prussia, she was a little over 250 years ago a small State under the suzerainty of the King of Poland; and six hundred years ago most of the Prussians proper were still heathens, talking a Slav language. It was only by the end of the thirteenth century that the *Prussi* were converted to Christianity.

Some South-German people contend that this conversion is not complete even in our days.

It is common knowledge that, of all the kinds of intractable pride, the pride of the upstart is the worst, the least amenable to sound limits. For centuries and centuries the Germans have been buffeted about by the French, English, Swedes, Poles, and formerly even by the Hungarians. For centuries the German Princes, hat in hand, went the round of all the Courts of Europe, begging for subsidies, kissing hands and licking shoes of various powerful ministers, mistresses, kings, popes and generals. For centuries they were used and utilised like so many flunkeys by the older and more powerful nations around them. The Prussian rulers especially, whether the so-called Great Elector, who died in 1688, or Frederick William I., in the eighteenth century, and Frederick William the Fourth in the nineteenth, were forced to eat many a humble pie and, as the French say, to swallow many a snake. Over one-half of the British State debt is composed of moneys thrown as sops, compensation, salaries, or bribes to innumerable German Princes during the seventeenth, eighteenth, and part of the nineteenth centuries.

As in matters of politics and State life, so it was also in matters of private life. Of all the nations of Europe, the Germans form the largest contingents of "foreigners" in various non-German countries. The Germans outside Germany and Austria are very much more numerous than either the Jews, the Chinese, or the gypsies. Millions of them are in America, in Russia, everywhere. Millions and millions of them are in the demoralising condition of expatriated, de-nationalized men and women. All that tells. All that leaves deep, indelible traces on the soul. It rankles in the heart; it embitters; it pricks and prods, until one day the mass of moral kindling takes fire, and then we have the prairie fire of a nation inflamed with a secular cry for vengeance, for the rehabilitation of their *status* as a nation and as individuals. It is a sort of *Jacquerie* or peasant-rising on a vast national scale. The peasants, too, after enduring all sorts of humiliation, finally rise, and then—woe to all humanity! Castles and their tenants are burned; men, women, and children are slaughtered. The human beast appears in its most hideous form.

The following incident has been told frequently enough; it can never be told too fre-

quently. When Adolphe Thiers, subsequently
President of the French Republic, went to the
various Courts of Europe, imploring them to
help France, which was then at the feet of the
victorious Germans, he met, at Vienna, the
German historian Ranke, the man who in his
numerous works had written up all the igno-
minies, humiliations, and indignities of German history. Thiers asked Ranke against
whom the Germans were fighting after Sedan,
since Napoleon III. was long their prisoner.
"Against whom?" Ranke exclaimed; "against
Louis XIV.!" Now, Louis XIV. died in 1715,
or over 150 years before the date of this conversation between Thiers and Ranke. Yet,
Ranke did not by any means exaggerate. The
humiliations inflicted upon the rulers of Germany by Louis XIV. had been so revolting that,
after five generations, the Germans were unable
to forget them. It was at the very palace of
Louis XIV. that the assembled German Princes
solemnly united in the establishment of the German Empire. The insult of 1681, when Louis
captured Strassburg in the midst of peace,
burned with the same fire in 1871. In fact, it
is only the common sense of the whole of German history to say that, for centuries, they were

accustomed to endure nameless insults at the hands of nearly all the nations around them, so that, whenever a Swedish or French conqueror spat into their faces, they exclaimed only: "Does it rain, I wonder!"

THE SAVIOURS OF THE WORLD

Now, let any one of some experience of life ask himself what may be expected from a person that has hitherto been lectured, insulted, and sweated by individuals whose superior he is now sure to be. It would surpass all human nature to keep one's head quite level under such circumstances. The Germans know that they are, or are held to be, the military superiors of any two or three of the nations surrounding them. Their innumerable writers, professors, journalists, poets, and politicians tell them so unceasingly, every day, in every paper, scientifically, learnedly, or philosophically. They hear that it was really they who saved the world in the past.

Just read the following extract from Chamberlain's book. He speaks of the wild Germans who invaded the Roman Empire. Of those savage hordes, Chamberlain says:—

"This barbarian, who prefers to enter the

battle naked, the savage, who suddenly rises up out of woods and marshes, to pour upon a civilised and cultivated world the horrors of a mighty conquest, and fights with the bare fist, is nevertheless the lawful heir of the Greek and the Roman, blood of their blood, and spirit of their spirit. What he unknowingly tears from strange hands is his own. But for him, the day of the Indo-European was passing to its end. The Asiatic and African slave had crept murderously up to the throne of the Roman Empire, while the Syrian bastard was seizing upon legislation, the Jew was using the library of Alexandria to adapt Greek philosophy to the Mosaic law; soon, too, the Mongolian was to crush under his savage blood-stained foot the sublime blossoms of the primal Aryan (*urarischen*) life: Indian thought, Indian poetry; and the Bedouin, intoxicated with the madness of devastation, was to burn that Garden of Eden, Erania, in which for thousands of years all the symbolism of the world had grown up, into an eternal desert; art had long ceased to exist, and there was for the rich only formality (*Schablonen*), for the poor circus-riding; therefore, to use Schiller's phrase, there were no longer men, but only creatures. It was high time that the deliverer appeared. . . . We can regret only one thing—that the German did not, everywhere his conquering arm preyed, exterminate more completely, and that, in consequence of this, the so-called Latinization, *i.e.*, the marriage with the chaos of peoples, gradually recovered wide territories from the only quickening influence of pure blood and unbroken youth, in fact, from the control of the highest talent.''

In other words, but for the Germans overrunning the Roman Empire—that is, but for this, the most unfortunate event of all European history—Europe could, so the Germans are now taught, never have been saved by ''the only quickening influence of pure blood and unbroken youth.'' Just think of the nonsense of it all! These ''fallen and corrupt'' Romans and Greeks forged, throughout the time when the ''pure and unbroken'' Germans invaded and ''saved'' them, the mightiest weapon of organisation and civilisation that had up to that time appeared in human history: the Roman Catholic Church. But for that Church and her redemption and colonisation of more than one-half of the soil of Europe, we should still, in company with the Germans, eat glands in the wild forests and swamps of Lancashire or Hanover.

But can any one wonder at this wholesale distortion of all history, when one reads what the contemporary German writers and thinkers and statesmen tell the Germans to think of themselves? The reader is asked to go patiently over the following extracts, and to consider that such excessive and wicked flattery is made to a nation that has, as we just saw, barely emerged out of a secular state of political inferiority. No more dangerous microbe could be implanted in the organism of a people.

Friedrich Lange, erstwhile editor of the *Tagliche Rundschau*, has gone so far as to invent and preach a species of "German religion" (*Deutsche Religion*), and from many pulpits it has been announced that "the German people is the elect of God, and its enemies are the enemies of the Lord."

Chamberlain teaches the Germans as follows:—"Who can live in Italy to-day and mix with its amiable and highly-gifted inhabitants without feeling with pain that here a great nation is lost, irredeemably lost, because it lacks the inner driving power, the greatness of soul, which would fit its talent? This power comes from Race alone. Italy had it as long as it possessed Germans: nay, even to-day, in those parts which were formerly occupied especially by Kelts, Germans, and Normans, the population develops the true German industry, and brings forth men who strive with desperate energy to keep the country together and to lead it in glorious paths. Cavour, the founder of the new kingdom, springs from the extreme North; Crispi, who knew how to steer it through dangerous rocks, from the extreme South.

"Fidelity is found in nearly all pure-bred races, *e.g.*, never more than in negroes; and what man could show more fidelity than the noble dog? This fidelity and that freedom do not grow one out of the other, but are two phenomena of the same character, of which one is more of the intellectual, the other more of the moral, side. The negro and the dog serve their master, whoever he is: that is the morality of the weak, or, as Aristotle has it, of him who is naturally born to be a slave. The German chooses his master, and therefore his fidelity is fidelity to himself: that is the morality of the free-born." For this reason, Chamberlain intimates, it is correct to consider St. Paul of German origin. This incredible freak of the perverted historical sense is put by Chamberlain in the following manner:—"More decisive for my theory is the kinship of the deeper spiritual dispositions between Kelts and Germans. . . . Does one, then, think it is a mere accident that St. Paul addressed his epistle on Redemption by Faith, etc., to the Galatians, to those Gallic Greeks of Asia Minor who had remained almost purely Keltic—that document in which one fancies one hears a German speaking who was exceptionally gifted for the understanding of deepest mysteries?"

Even the wild Goths were noble and tolerant, according to Herr Chamberlain, and therefore superior to the foul Romans:—"Thus the perfect religious tolerance of the Goths, when they became masters of that Roman Empire in which the principle of intolerance had so long prevailed, is as characteristic of German feeling as is the protection which they gave to the monuments of art. We see here those two features: fidelity and freedom. . . . The German is the most ideal, and at the same time the most practical, man in the world, and that, not because these are contrasts, but because they are identical. The German writes *'Die Kritik der reinen Vernunft,'* but invents at the same time the railway; the century of Bessemer and Edison is that of Beethoven and R. Wagner."

Their writers tell the Germans:—"We are the best colonists, the best sailors, and even the best merchants. . . . We are the most intelligent nation there is, and the most advanced in science and art. . . . We are, without contradiction, the most warlike people on earth."

The sense and passion of everything German are carried to such an extent that Bismarck's secretary once wrote to the Municipal Council of Berlin:—

"I have the honour, on behalf of Prince Bismarck, to thank the Municipal Council of the Royal City of Berlin for the transmission of a pamphlet relating to the fifty-ninth meeting of German doctors and naturalists. His Highness regrets, however, that he is unable to take cognisance of it, as his principles forbid his reading a German text printed in Latin characters.

"V. REINBABEN."

The astonishment of the Municipal Council of Berlin was pretty great on receiving this let-

ter. It became immense when it was noticed
that the printed heading of the letter was alone
in Latin characters.

GERMANY AND THE FUTURE

Can one wonder, under such circumstances,
that the Kaiser a few years ago, at the cele-
bration of the 200th anniversary of the foundation of the Kingdom of Prussia, exclaimed:
"Nothing must be settled in this world without the intervention of Germany and of the
German Emperor."

In 1905, the Kaiser, on the 28th of April, a
few days after the conclusion of the Anglo-
French *Entente Cordiale,* said, at Carlsruhe:
"Let us remember the great time in which German unity was established on the fields of
Woerth, Weissemburg, and Sedan. Present
events invite us to forget internal discords.
Let us be united in case we should be compelled
to intervene in the politics of the world." On
1st May at Mayence, at the opening of a new
bridge, he said: "This work, destined to develop peaceful communications, might serve for
graver purposes."

After such utterances on the part of a responsible ruler, we need not be astonished to

learn that irresponsible professors, whose influence on the Germans is nevertheless extraordinary, indulge in far louder dreams. Thus Professor Treitschke, the most jingoist of all German historians, and also one of their ablest writers, says:—

"Then, when the German flag flies over and protects this vast Empire, to whom will belong the sceptre of the universe? What nation will impose its wishes on the other enfeebled and decadent people? Will it not be Germany that will have the mission to ensure the peace of the world? Russia, that immense colossus still in process of formation, and with feet of clay, will be absorbed in its home and economic difficulties. England, stronger in appearance than in reality, will, without any doubt, see her Colonies detach themselves from her and exhaust themselves in fruitless struggles. France, given over to internal dissensions and the strife of parties, will sink into hopeless decadence. As to Italy, she will have her work cut out to ensure a crust of bread to her children. . . . The future belongs to Germany, to which Austria will attach herself if she wishes to survive."

It is under the pressure of such ideas, taught in Germany by their foremost writers and thinkers, that the Germans have persuaded themselves of the necessity of occupying vast territories, both in their own neighbourhood and in foreign continents. This Greater Germany, or the expansion of the German race (as if such a thing existed—as if the Germans had not the blood of all the nations in them) has become a dogma with the Germans. Even in their school books it is publicly taught. See the following from the manual of Herr Daniel, professor of geography at the Royal College at Halle:—

"France was primarily a small kingdom born of the dismemberment of Charlemagne's empire and bounded by the Rhone and the Saône rivers, and has only expanded at the expense of Germany; during the Middle Ages Lyons and Marseilles were German towns."

The same author, in an equally classical work in use in the schools, gives the "natural frontiers of Germany as on the west" are "the hills which extend from Cape Grisnez to the Argonne, the plateau of Langres, the *faucilles*, the mountains of Alsace, the heights between the Rhine and the Rhone, and the Jura to the lake of Geneva."

If Germans are taught similar political

geography about France, the reader may easily imagine what they are given to understand about the "inevitable" destiny of the smaller Slav peoples in their neighbourhood. Thus we read in Pan-German books:—

"We sometimes hear the following objection from the savants and sages, opponents of the Pan-Germanic idea. 'Of what use to us will be the Czechs, the Slovenians, and the others? Will the Catholics of Austria really represent an increase of our power?' To the first objection we reply that a universal Germany is only possible if the great Slav power Russia is crumbled to bits, is completely overthrown. Then, when the triumphant German armies occupy the country from the Moldau to the Adriatic, it will be possible simply to expel the non-German populations from Cisleithania. . . . An indemnity may be given them, but the country must be cleared and the land colonised by Germans. In the event of such momentous happenings, we would not hesitate to take large tracts of territory from France and Russia to form the glacis of our frontiers on the east and on the west. It would, moreover, be necessary to impose as a condition of peace that the native should evacuate these provinces and be

compensated by the conquered powers. There
again colonisation would be carried out. That
is how we propose to enlarge our European
frontiers. This enlargement has become for
us a matter of necessity, just as bread is necessary for our rapidly increasing population."

The *Vorwärts* has put it on record that, to a
numerous and sympathetic audience of professors and students of Protestant Theology,
the theologian Lezius made a speech, which was
loudly applauded, in which he advised that the
Prussian Poles should be treated like Chinamen. The following is an extract from this
prodigious oration:—

"Solomon has said: 'Do not be too good;
do not be too just.' The Polish press should
be simply annihilated. All Polish societies
should be suppressed, without the slightest
apology being made for such a measure. This
summary procedure should be likewise applied
to the French and Danish press, as well as to
the societies of Alsace, Lorraine, and Schleswig-
Holstein. Especially should no consideration
whatever be shown to anything relating to the
Poles. The Constitution should be altered with
regard to the latter. The Poles should be
looked upon as helots. They should be allowed

but three privileges: to pay taxes, serve in the army, and shut their jaws" (*sic*).

In the following extracts the reader may follow the various stages of that German expansion all over the globe.

Schmoller, the political economist, writes:—"We must at all costs hope for the formation in *Southern Brazil,* of a state with 20 or 30 million Germans, and that this State should remain an integral part of Brazil, whether it be constituted as an independent state, or whether it remain in close relation with the Empire." He quotes from *Deutsches Handels Archiv,* March, 1901, a report of the German Consul at Blumenau (Brazil):—"Of the 40,000 inhabitants, about 30,000 are German Brazilians, 8,000 are Austrians, and the residue is composed of Portuguese Brazilians." He quotes Dr. Hasse as saying: "We shall see the German oak grow bigger, and from the German Emperor will spring the Emperor of the Germans." Schmoller quotes also from *Handelsmuseum,* June 13, 1901:—"Little by little, slowly and surely, Germany is securing the trade of *Bolivia.* When she has done that entirely, she will have secured the plenitude of influence, a complete moral and material supremacy, and a colony acquired without war or expense.''

The German military authorities add:—''The German army and fleet must have at command a field where they can work homogeneously. If, as seems probable, the work of the army should be to the south and east of the Empire, it is almost indispensable that it should be supported by the fleet in the Adriatic and the Mediterranean. Our strategic front must extend from the Baltic to Trieste. France and Russia have each a share in the maintenance of equilibrium in the seas of North Europe and of the Mediterranean Basin. We must have exactly the same. Besides, are the shores of the Upper Adriatic so far from German lands? There is little more than 100 kilometres as the crow flies from the Gulf of Trieste to the frontier of South Carinthia—a point from which, going northward and skirting Bohemia, there are nothing but compact masses of Germans to be found. On no account should this part of the coast be allowed to fall into Latin or Slav hands, for, if it were, that side of Germany is swamped for a century, maybe for ever.''

The Japanese talk hopefully of conquering the *Dutch East Indies,* which they consider an easy prey; and the Germans, on their side, confidently remark that if the lesser Holland of Europe became a dependence of the Great Empire, the greater Holland of the Antipodes would become the finest of the German colonies.

At *Kiao-chau* the Emperor William had given a first exhibition of his attitude towards China. Glorying in his strength, and impatient to parade it, looking on the Chinese as a "barbaric people," he extolled the "mailed fist" and encouraged it among his representatives. Baron Ketteler paid with his life for his imprudence and his provocations. Personally hit by the assassination of his minister, the Emperor seized the occasion to adopt a tragic attitude; in his imagination he saw himself a new Joshua, fighting with the people of God, against the Amalekites, and at the same time—with that curious mixture of practical common sense and romantic imagination which is one of the characteristic traits of his nature—started a diplomatic campaign for the acceptance of a German field-marshal as head of the international army.

In *Western Asia* the Germans pursue, and

not unsuccessfully, a forward policy of constant infiltration. The following extracts are very instructive.

Lt.-Col. Hildebrandt writes: "The Germans likewise have a great strategic interest in the *Bagdad Railway,* for in the contingent event of a blockade of the Suez Canal—a blockade which political complications, or, later on, military operations, might bring within the range of possibilities—this railway would supply Germany with the most direct road to the East of Africa and Asia and towards her transoceanic possessions."

Siegmund Schneider writes in *Die Deutsche Bagdadbahn:* "Russia has, by the treaty of St. Petersburg of 1896, secured the right to send along the railway lines of Eastern China (covering 1,500 kilometres of Chinese Manchuria) detachments of Siberian Cossacks to guard their line. In the same way it will be necessary, during the construction of the Bagdad Railway, that similar measures should be carried out to ensure the safety of the constructors and protect them from the attacks of Bedouins and brigands in Kurdistan, Mesopotamia, and Babylonia."

Dr. Rohrbach writes in *Die Bagdadbahn:*

"A Turkey strong, militarily and politically, can alone enable us to find in the lands of the Euphrates and the Tigris an increase of our national possessions and an improvement in the economic scale. For a weak Turkey not a *pfennig,* but to a strong Turkey let us give all the money that may be required."

Dr. Paul Rohrbach writes in *Die Zeit:* "There can no longer be any doubt on the subject. The Anatolia Railway Co., which is in the hands of the *Deutsche Bank* of Berlin, will have the financial and technical management of the undertaking. It may, therefore, be said that the Bagdad Railway is in reality a German enterprise, as we on our side desired it to be and strove to make it, whilst our adversaries on the other hand did their utmost to thwart it at Constantinople with so much jealousy and tenacity."

Lt.-Col. Hildebrandt, writing in the *Internationale Revue über die gesammten Armeen und Flotten* (p. 73, March, 1902), Witzleben, Dresden, says: "The concession was granted at the end of 1899, and it may be taken that it was obtained thanks to the policy of the German Government, which has resolutely claimed for its country the position of a world-power in the concert of nations. The construction of the line is consequently in German hands; and the same is the case with the huge maritime works which are being carried out by the Anatolia Company on a site which will furnish an excellent port, and in the Bay of Ismid, on the spot known as Haidar-Pasha, near Scutari, on the Bosphorus, opposite to Constantinople, of which it may be said to form a suburb.''

At the end of March, 1902, the following note appeared in the Turkish papers:—''Up till to-day MM. Zander (representing the *Deutsche Bank*) and Huguenin have acted as managing directors of the Anatolia Railway. Henceforth M. Zander will take up the title and duties of 'Manager of the New Concession Lines,' and M. Huguenin remains manager of the Anatolia Company.''

In 1880 the trade of Germany with the Ottoman Empire amounted to 8,500,000 francs (£340,000); in 1900 it had increased to 81,250,-000 francs (£3,250,000); and in 1904 to 84,450,-000 francs (£3,378,000), having increased tenfold in twenty years.

This regular system of expansion is very considerable, aided by various societies whose only aim is the spread of the German language,

of German commerce, and German ideas.
Thus, the *Allgemeiner Deutscher Sprachverein*
sends subsidies to the German schools scattered
throughout the world, and especially to those
in the Slav countries of Austria; the Society
for the Propagation of the German Language
(*Deutscher Sprachverein*) works in the same di-
rection. The *Deutsche Kolonial Gesellschaft*
encourages ideas of oversea expansion, whilst
the *Deutscher Flottenverein,* with already close
on 1,000,000 members, completes the work of
converting public opinion to new sacrifices so
as to have by 1915 a fleet strong enough to beat
the British fleet. It is especially religious societies that distinguish themselves by their zeal.
The *Odin-Verein* of Munich, the *Gustav-Adolf
Verein* have specially devoted themselves to
the "evangelisation" of Austria; the arrest of
one of their missionaries, pastor Everling,
caused some sensation at the time. The *Evan-
gelical League* has conducted with great ardour
the *"Los von Rom"* ("Away from Rome!")
campaign, for which in 1903 it had already dis-
bursed 400,000 marks. All seem to fulfil a
sacred function, the exaltation of the national
name and greatness. "The king at the head

of Prussia, Prussia at the head of Germany, Germany at the head of the world.''

Such nations as the Germans cannot reasonably hope to absorb, they unremittingly endeavour to win over to their interests. Amongst these the Americans proper, the people of the United States, are the foremost. The Kaiser rarely misses an opportunity of ingratiating himself with the Yankees. He sent their universities works of art; he introduced the flourishing system of a constant exchange of professors, so that American professors are giving temporarily lectures at Berlin, while German scholars go to the States to deliver discourses on German Science; now, he is said to send one of his sons to Princeton University to be educated in America; he has recently utilised the chance left him by the oversight of the British Government, and sent an official representative to the solemn opening of the Carnegie Institute at Pittsburg. More than this is done by a host of German writers, who submit to the Americans tempting reflections such as the following:—

''The apprehensions of the American people prevent the United States establishing compul-

sory military service; they can only rely, therefore, on the development of their navy. The
most rational solution for the United States is,
therefore, to seek a *'rapprochement'* with Germany. The strength of the combined fleets will
soon exceed that of the British Navy. On the
other hand, the magnificent German army would
render possible widespreading transoceanic ex-
peditions. . . . The similarity of character fa-
vours a German-American alliance. Our sixty
million citizens and the eighty million American
are ever increasing and multiplying, and see
their qualities improve, whereas the Latin races
remain stationary or retrograde. Thus the
Teutonic race, to which Americans belong as
well as ourselves, could aspire to the domina-
tion of the globe if the two nations walked together instead of remaining isolated. Since
1820 Germany has sent over five million emi-
grants to the United States, that is, 22 per
cent. of the total immigration. No other country has sent so large a contingent. At the last
census (1900) the number of individuals settled in the United States born to two German
parents or one was estimated at 7,800,000, and
of this number over two and a half millions had
been born in Germany."

THE COMING STRUGGLE

From the preceding extracts it will be seen that the Germans are now suffused with a profound and passionate belief in their great historical vocation. Again and again we beg to submit to the British reader that he must not take views and opinions such as have been here given in the way in which such things are taken by the nation of the United Kingdom. In Great Britain all sorts of views and intellectual or political opinions are constantly being published and discussed; yet, with the exception of a few faddists and eccentrics, nobody takes them over-seriously. At any rate, it may be stated with absolute correctness that very few people in this country are likely to labour any given political or economical theory to its logical extremes.

The British nation has grappled with the realities of politics, party strifes, international policy, or ordinary wealth far too much to be addicted to mere theoretical pushing of ideas to their inferential fag ends. Hence the most extreme ideas in religion, philosophy, or politics are, in Great Britain, less likely to be carried out in unmodified strict logic. Compro-

mise and half-measure wisdom are the soul of
this country. In Germany, on the other hand,
imperial problems, for instance, are as yet
purely theoretic. No Germans, if we except
one or two generations of Germans, have ever
had any practical acquaintance with imperial
problems. They cannot, therefore, know how
to fit ideas to reality, how to modify theory to
practice. Under these circumstances, their
theoretic bent has all but free scope. Where,
in reality, there are a thousand difficulties, they
see none. The whole matter of world-power
appears to them in the light of a simple and
clear problem. The opinions of their leaders
are taken by the Germans quite literally, and
the realisation of their unbounded ambition is,
they hold, only a matter of a few sound laws
and increased energy.

All this only adds to the overweening conceit
filling them. For, not only are they convinced
that the world ought to be theirs, but also that
this appropriation of the globe, and perhaps
of a few other planets, is relatively a simple
affair. They, therefore, do not hesitate to draw
the logical conclusion from all that their leaders tell them. One has only to read the following speech by Gen. Von der Goltz:—

"It is therefore necessary to convince ourselves, and to convince the generation we have
to educate, that the time for rest has not yet
arrived; that the prediction of a *supreme struggle,* in which the existence and the power of
Germany will be at stake, is by no means a
vain chimera emanating from the imaginations
of a few ambitious madmen; that this supreme
struggle will burst forth one day terrible and
momentous as all struggles between nations
that serve as a prelude to great political revolutions."

Also, Gen. Bernhardi's speech to the Berlin
Society, 23rd January, 1905:—"In spite of
treaties and peace congresses, it is still by steel
that great questions are settled."

"The English peril haunts Germany," writes
M. Georges Villiers. "By the force of things
the 20th century will see the German and the
Anglo-Saxon in a death struggle for maritime
and commercial supremacy. At any rate, there
is hardly a German who is not persuaded to-
day that such will be the case. Those even who
deny the possibility of such a conflict are not
those whom it preoccupies least."

And Prince Bülow, the German Chancellor,
in a speech delivered in the Reichstag (Decem-

ber 6th, 1897), said:—"The time has gone by
when Germans left the earth to one of their
neighbours and the sea to another, retaining
for themselves the sky, where pure doctrine
reigns."

As a corroboration of the statement here
made with regard to the extraordinarily high-
strung feeling of imperial expansion on the part
of the Germans, we here add two remarks made
by well-known men in the world of literature,
one a French Catholic priest, the other a Russian novelist. The Père Didon, author of several famous works on Jesus and the religious
movement of our day, says:—

"She (Germany) lays claim to being militarily, politically, scientifically, religiously,
morally, and *cerebrally* the first nation in the
world. Chauvinism in Germany is more than
a sentiment; it is a theory, a dogma in a scientific dress. A distinction is made between
the two races, the German and the Latin; the
German, although only a newcomer on the scene
where great events are enacted, being naturally
placed first."

The Russian novelist, Dostoïewski, writes:—
"Chauvinism, pride, and an unlimited confi-
dence in their own strength have intoxicated the

Germans since the war. This people, that has so rarely been a conqueror and has so often been conquered, had all of a sudden beaten the nation that had humiliated all the other nations. . . . On the other hand, the fact that Germany, but yesterday all parcelled out, has been able in so short a time to develop so strong a political organisation, might well lead the Germans to believe that they are about to enter on a new phase of brilliant development. This conviction has resulted in making the German not only Chauvinistic and conceited, but flighty as well; it is not only the Teutonic grocer and shoemaker now who are over-confident, but professors, eminent scientists, and even the ministers themselves as well.''

No wonder that the arrogance of the ''Elect Ones of God'' come out at every possible and impossible occasion. When Bismarck was asked what he would do, should some 100,000 British soldiers be landed on the north coast of Germany in case of a war between Great Britain, France and Germany, he replied: ''I should have them arrested by the police.''

PART II

IN the preceding section of this work something was said about the notions of extreme national pride and jingoism with which a very great and exceedingly influential number of German writers, thinkers, professors, statesmen, and journalists have these twenty odd years filled the heads of the Germans. This by itself is, we venture to submit, a dangerous state of things, and we have repeatedly tried to explain to the reader how these fanatic articles, books, views, or utterances of German leading men must be taken at their full face value, and how absurd it would be to compare their effect upon the German nation with that of similar books in this country.

Everybody has heard of the vast influence which, in the eighteenth century, was exercised by a handful of French writers about political economy and politics on the coming and on the character of the French Revolution. One cannot, indeed, maintain that History is always governed by ideas, and thus by thinkers and writers. But there are periods and conditions when such otherwise harmless multipliers of ink factories have a very serious influence upon their nation.

In this chapter we are going to put before the reader the various circumstances which, independently of what German writers think or say, have powerfully contributed to swell the German head.[1]

Common sense—the least common of things, though the most necessary—will tell any man who gives his thoughts to matters of European history and politics that no single nation in Europe can be great or small but what the other nations contribute to it very considerably. A self-made nation does not exist any more than does, strictly speaking, a self-made man. Some other nation has invariably had a hand in it. So we note that Spanish greatness was grafted and partly caused by the weak-

[1] Although Germany's struggle for supremacy has been precipitated in a manner that Dr. Reich could not foresee, and some of his hypotheses and deductions are correspondingly irrelevant to the present European crisis, there is yet left in this and the succeeding section of his work much that is valuable in the matters of information and criticism. We venture to think that these sections are still worthy of perusal, before the reader passes to the Epitome in which the case stated by Dr. Reich in his first section is manifestly confirmed.—Ed.

ness of the then Germany and Italy. French greatness in the seventeenth century was based on the then weakness of Spain, Italy, Germany, and, periodically, of England, too. At present (1907) Germany's greatness, which is undeniable, is based on the partial eclipse of France and Austria and on the absence of the spirit of Chatham in England.

It is unnecessary to refer here to diplomatic and other incidents which have served to obscure the importance of France in comparison with Germany. We proceed to consider the position of Austria-Hungary.

AUSTRIA-HUNGARY VASSAL OF GERMANY

In the case of Austria-Hungary, things stand even much better for a mushroom-growth of the German swelled-head. There is, in fact, no exaggeration in saying that Austria-Hungary is, in international politics, the mere vassal of Germany. For over two centuries the rulers of Prussia were the humble subordinates of the Austrian Hapsburgs. When, at the beginning of the eighteenth century, the Electors of Brandenburg became Kings of Prussia, they became so by the grace of the Austrian rulers, who were the Emperors of the Holy Roman

Empire. As late as 1850 the King of Prussia was slighted, not to say duped, by the ruler of Austria. Since 1866 this has been completely reversed. Not only was Austria signally defeated by Prussia in that year; but when, in 1870, Germany made war on France, and Austria thereby had an excellent opportunity of squaring her count with Germany, the Austrians did not do so at all, and thus missed the greatest of their chances in modern history. Ever since, Austria-Hungary has been, in her own self-interest, bound to make friends with Germany, to abet and follow her, or to be, as was said above, her vassal.

At the conference of Algeciras, for the settlement of the Moroccan Question, when all the other Powers sided with France and England, Austria-Hungary went, arm in arm, with Germany. Things have come to such a pass that Germany is at present the strongest guarantee for the maintenance of the dual empire called Austria-Hungary. The author, himself a Hungarian, is well aware of the fact that nine persons out of ten in this country indulge in the belief that Austria-Hungary will, on the demise of Francis Joseph I., who is now (May, 1907) seventy-six years old, fall to pieces, and that the Germans will take up and assimilate as many of these pieces as they may care to.

This belief is, we venture to submit, totally erroneous. On the demise of her present aged ruler, Austria-Hungary will not fall to pieces at all. That dual empire is a peculiar product, the oddest of European history. It has no unity whatever, racial, national, religious, or geographical. It is, in one word, not a straightforward, natural result of the energy and the opportunities of a people, such as is France, England, or Germany; it is a makeshift, a *pis-aller,* as the French call it; a thing which is bad enough as it is, but the absence of which would be worse still. Old Palacky, the historian of the Bohemians or Czechs, rightly said that if Austria did not exist, it would be necessary to invent it. It is not a country, or a nation; it is a misfortune, but an inevitable one. This can be made clear very briefly.

The Germans have had too many terrible disasters in the last three centuries; they have, as was pointed out above, learned too many a wholesome lesson, to ignore what a blind man can see. We mean, they know that any attempt of theirs on a Continental country, unless really justified as an act of self-defence, would almost immediately call forth a coalition of most of the other Powers of Europe. Suppose, for instance, that Germany, out of sheer arrogance and greed, should invade Holland or Switzerland. Nothing can be surer than that such an invasion would at once prevail upon the other Continental Powers to unite against Germany. If Germany should, instead of Holland or Switzerland, choose Austria as an object of appropriation, the balance of power would be thereby so gravely affected that Italy and France, let alone Hungary, Belgium, and Holland, would forthwith combine for the rehabilitation of the European equilibrium.

All this the Germans know full well. Their leaders, such as Professor Hans Delbrück, tell them so every day. They do not want to repeat the fatal mistake of Napoleon. The great French Emperor was almost unceasingly making war on one Continental Power after the other, until finally all of them coalesced and combined against him, and so brought about his downfall. The Germans are quite aware that if, trusting in their superior military organisation, they continue exasperating one Con-

tinental nation after the other, those nations
will without fail unite against them, and fight
them until they meet their Waterloo.

Quite apart from this danger of a European,
at any rate a Continental, coalition against
them, the more thoughtful of the Germans are
not at all anxious to absorb recalcitrant nations
on the Continent. Already the few million
Poles cause them no end of trouble; and if the
Germans, by hypothesis, forced the Dutch,
Swiss, let alone the Austrians, into the German Empire, their Imperial Parliament would
become a real *inferno,* or, in plain English, an
ungovernable anarchy. Prince Bülow, the German Chancellor, has repeatedly declared that
the Poles form the greatest danger to the German Empire. Now, fancy some nine million
Catholic Austrians entering the German Empire, and thus, by their deputies, the German
Imperial Parliament. The Catholic or Centre
Party is already one of the most influential
parties in the *Reichstag* at Berlin; if nine million more Catholics should be represented in
it, the Catholics would swamp the German Parliament. The Germans, mostly Protestant, cannot possibly desire that. Bismarck said more

than once that he could not afford to absorb
Austria, even if it were offered to him.

GERMAN "WORLD-POLICY"

All the foregoing reasons do not as yet give
the complete statement with regard to Germany's unwillingness to seize on Austria.
There is a still more powerful reason; one
which at this stage of our little work we cannot
discuss in full, but which may and must be
touched upon. It is this: What Germany
wants and desires is not continental expansion,
but maritime expansion. In seizing part of
Austria, the Germans would, to put it in simple
language, only catch a Tartar. The gain is
doubtful, the advantage far from certain. To
expand on sea, on the other hand, would give
the Germans unbounded facilities for their
ever-growing surplus population, and for their
international trade. If we suppose that Germany is offered the choice between say, Switzerland and South Africa; there is no doubt whatever that the Germans would select the latter.
In the same way, Asia-Minor has immense at-
tractions for them; and the Dutch islands in
the East Indies are an object fervently desired

by Germany. All this transmarine expansion,
however, means sea-power; in fact, supremacy
on the sea. This supremacy, again, means a
victorious war with Great Britain.

This, then, is the real, the true, the only objective of German "world-policy." If Great
Britain yielded to them, by force of course, her
supremacy on sea, the Germans would not trouble much longer about being aggressive on the
Continent. It would not pay them. To wrest
the naval supremacy from Britain is a matter
of war, but of a war incomparably shorter and
less costly than a war with a continental coalition. It is well known that naval campaigns
may be decided in an exceedingly short time,
in a week or two. One signal victory, and the
campaign is decided. Such a rapid solution of
the problem cannot be so much as dreamed of
on the Continent. On the other hand, neither
Britain nor Germany can seriously hope to be
joined, in a naval war, by a coalition proper.
No more disastrous mistake can be made than
to believe that Britain will eventually be helped
by France, that is, by the French fleet. It will
not, unless a very profound and improbable
change comes over the whole mind of the French
nation.

The Germans would therefore have to face the British fleet alone. This is undoubtedly a considerable venture. Yet it cannot be compared with the venture of facing a Continental coalition against the German army. If the British nation had attacked Germany a few years ago, say at the time of the Kaiser's telegram to Krüger, the ambition of the Germans with regard to maritime expansion would have been nipped in the bud. At that time the disproportion between the British and the German fleets was too much in favour of the former. In a few years' time, however, this disproportion will be very much toned down. Unless one believes in the absolute and unconditional invincibility of the British fleet as in a sort of law of nature, one is not entitled to assume that the German fleet cannot ever defeat it. Such statements may do in public gatherings crowned by a wildly jingoistic gallery. They cannot be taken seriously in a study of Britain's future. At any rate, it remains true that the Germans are entitled to think that it is much easier and more profitable to make good their desire for maritime expansion than to realise any hope of absorbing the Continent against a coalition of Powers. In the former case they would have

to fight only one, if a very great, Power; in
the latter they would be attacked by at least
ten Powers.

Given all these undeniable circumstances, no
sane person will lightly attribute to the Germans an idea of beginning their expansion by
an attack on a great and hitherto friendly Continental Power, such as Austria-Hungary.
Quite on the contrary: Since the Germans are
fully aware of the folly of rousing against
themselves, unnecessarily, some 150,000,000
continentals; since, moreover, transmarine expansion is for them by far the more profitable
expansion of the two, and by far the more feasible, the Germans will, there is not a shadow of a
doubt, take great care to avoid any complications on the Continent. They will do everything in their power to maintain the chief Continental State in the centre of Europe, that is,
Austria-Hungary.

That legend of the disruption and collapse
of Austria-Hungary after the death of the present ruler is only a thought whose parent is the
wish of the, alas! but too numerous, peace-at-
any-pricers of this country. In their humanity
they wish the Germans to ravage, occupy, and
swallow Austria-Hungary, instead of attacking

the British fleet. Such an Austrian diversion,
those goody-goody ones think in the inmost
recesses of their hearts, would keep the obnox-
ious Teuton from the shores of this country.
So it would, but the Germans are not kind
enough to be made the cat's-paw of Exeter
Hall, and of the members of the Society for
the Prevention of Cruelty to Cats.

It has so far been shown that the extraordinary self-assurance of the Germans is partly
based on the eclipse of France and of Austria-
Hungary. We shall now see that Russia, too,
by her complete defeat at the hands of the
Japanese and by the ensuing anarchy within
her empire, has for the time being ceased to
have any serious influence on European matters. If one considers that it was the German
Kaiser who, practically the first, in a now famous painting of his, foreshadowed the "Yellow Peril," and that this very "Yellow Peril"
was the cause of the downfall of Russia, and
thus of the unprecedented ascendency of Germany, one cannot but be amazed at the strange
and contradictory effects of political events.
Russia is not only the immediate neighbour of
Germany; there is also practically no natural
barrier of any serious kind between the two

countries. This has always rendered Germany very apprehensive of danger on the Eastern or Russian side of her empire. It has repeatedly prevailed upon German rulers to go warily and with even exaggerated caution. It has, under all circumstances, poured water into the German wine, as the French say. They could not think of sounding high trumpet-tones in handling international affairs. The Russian Bear was there. But now (1907) he is no longer there. He has withdrawn into his obscure lair, there to lick his own wounds, a-grumbling and a-moaning.

THE POSITION IN 1907

If, then, we twine up all the threads of European politics into one big rope of inference, it comes to this: In all Europe there is at present no longer a concert of six great Powers, but only a duo of two Powers: Germany and Great Britain. The rest of the Powers are what in music we call *ripieni,* i.e., merely filling out the chords and harmonies. This state of minored prestige Germany has a capital interest to maintain in Europe. If the politically anæmic Powers should coalesce and unite against Germany, they might become most dangerous to Germany. Hence the whole of German policy is directed to one single object: to keep the former great Powers as bloodless as possible, to anæmiate without unduly exasperating them. This done, there remains for the Germans one single great duel, that with Great Britain. This, they hope they will be able to manage.

The reader has undoubtedly noticed, from time to time, the progress in building men-of-war that has, in the course of the last ten years, been made in Germany. The daily papers bring such reports from authentic sources, and here and there a more thoughtful Englishman has collected them for future reference. The mass of this nation, we are afraid, has treated these most serious matters with the usual levity. It is, therefore, necessary to collect here the latest and most authentic data about the startling progress of the German fighting navy, in order to impress the British reader with the fact above insisted upon, to wit, that the Germans do prepare for a possible encounter with Great Britain. Their navy can have only one meaning: England, or, to speak with due regard to Scots and Irish, let alone Welsh susceptibilities, Great Britain. Neither Russia

nor Denmark, Norway or Sweden are threatening the German coast. The colonies of the
Germans are primitive; and their trade does
not as yet require a navy as vast as the one
they are building. Now, as to the facts of their
men-of-war, built and building:

During 1906 the German navy was increased
by fifteen new warships, all of which were built
in German shipbuilding yards, and represent a
total displacement of 62,582 tons. Only three
of these warships were built in the Government
yards, and it speaks volumes for the gradual
development of shipbuilding in Germany that
the remaining twelve units were turned out by
private yards. These fifteen units were made
up of two squadron-battleships, two armoured-
cruisers, two small cruisers, one mine-laying
vessel, one ship for hydrographical purposes,
one tender, six torpedo-boats, and one submarine; one of the torpedo-boats has not been
launched yet. The battleships were the *Schle-
sien,* launched at Danzig in May, and the
Schleswig-Holstein, launched in December at
Gaarden, near Kiel; each is of 13,200 tons, and
they are the last of the five vessels of the
Deutschland type. With these two, the German
navy has now twenty-four big battleships.

The armoured cruisers are the *Scharnhorst,* launched at Hamburg in March, and the *Gneisenau,* launched in June at Gropelingen, on the Weser; each is of 11,500 tons displacement. The small cruiser *Nürnberg* was launched at Kiel in August, and the *Stuttgart* at Danzig in September. The *Nautilus,* Germany's first mine-layer, of 2,000 tons, was launched on the Weser in August; the tender *Delphin,* of 445 tons, was launched at Kiel in January. One division of torpedo-boats was launched at Kiel; the last of these boats, *G 137,* fitted with the Parsons turbines, and of 572 tons could not be launched in December, nor has the date yet been fixed. Finally, last August, the *U 1,* the first submarine boat owned by Germany, was launched from the Krupp Germania yard at Gaarden; it is of 180 tons.

In an appendix to Count Reventlow's book, *"Weltfrieden oder Weltkrieg"* (*World-peace or World-war*), 1907, the well-known German writer on naval subjects gives an interesting account of his correspondence with six of the most important private shipbuilding yards in Germany with regard to their resources for the construction of battleships and cruisers of the largest type. Krupp's Germania yards at Kiel replied that they were perfectly capable of completing a large battleship or cruiser within a period of twenty-four to thirty months, and that the seven slip-ways at their disposal would enable them to lay down at least two of these vessels every year. The Howaldts works, also of Kiel, returned a similar reply, and guaranteed to deliver one large battleship or cruiser every year after the first two years. The mechanical appliances available at Kiel were of the most modern type, and skilled labour was plentiful. The Vulkan yards at Stettin stated that they could lay down two battleships of 18,000 tons each and two cruisers of 15,000 tons every year. If the guns and armour were promptly delivered by the makers, they too would be able to complete the ships within twenty-four to thirty months. When the Vulkan's new yards at Hamburg had been opened their productive capacity would be increased 50 to 75 per cent. The firm of Blohm and Voss estimated that they could lay down two large ships, either battleships or cruisers, every year, and that they could deliver them within two or two and a half years if a continuous succession of orders were assured. Herr Schichau, of Schichau's works at Danzig and Elbing, re-

plied that, if necessary, he could "comfort-
ably" accommodate four battleships of 18,000
tons each upon the stocks, and could also at
the same time carry on the work of fitting out
two or three more similar vessels. Herr
Schichau informed Count Reventlow that he
had already completed a battleship in thirty
months, but that in general he would prefer to
receive a fresh order every half-year rather
than reduce the present building period of
thirty to thirty-six months, which was quite
short enough. The Weser Shipbuilding Company drew attention to its new yards, and
pledged its ability to lay down two battleships
and two cruisers simultaneously, and to complete them within a period of twenty-four to
thirty months. In addition to these private
yards, Germany possesses all the resources of
the Imperial navy yards at Kiel and Wilhelmshaven.

The extent of dock accommodation for large
ships available in German ports is described
as being ample, so that from this point of view
there is no reason why the rate of construction
for the German navy should not be accelerated.
There are four floating docks, including one
with a capacity of 35,000 tons, at Hamburg, one

at Bremen, and one at Stettin, all of which are in private hands, while the naval authorities have two dry docks at Kiel and four at Wilhelmshaven, two of which are still under construction. The State of Bremen also owns a dry dock at Bremerhaven, which is rented by the North-German Lloyd, and, if necessary, the locks of the Kiel Canal could be utilised for docking large ships, especially when the new and larger locks which are projected have been built.

Furthermore, we read the following telling facts in April, 1906:—

The action of the German Admiralty in placing with extreme promptitude the orders for the two new battleships to be laid down under the German programme of 1907 has come as something of a surprise to the British naval authorities. The large armoured ships to be laid down for the German Navy this year are three in number. Two of them are described as battleships and the other is known as an armoured cruiser. All three are larger than any vessels yet built or designed for the British Navy. The two battleships will displace 19,-000 metric tons, or 18,000 British tons, apiece, 800 tons larger than the Dreadnought. It is understood that they will be laid down in the next few weeks. Their armament is reported to be fourteen or sixteen 11-in. guns of fifty calibres, so mounted that they will bring to bear a broadside superior to that of the Dreadnought. They will, it is believed, have turbine engines, though, since great secrecy has been maintained as to their details, nothing is certainly known. Their speed will probably be about the same as that of the Dreadnought. They will be completed in the summer of 1910.

The new German armoured cruiser will displace about 19,200 tons, and will therefore be 2,000 tons larger than the British ships of the Invincible class. It is known that she will have turbine engines and that a speed of over twenty-five knots is expected from her. Her armament is believed to consist of ten 11-in. guns mounted in the centre line, so that all can fire on either broadside, but some accounts represent it as being even more powerful. Like the British Invincibles, she will be capable of destroying any battleship of the pre-Dreadnought era.

In all, this summer (1907) Germany will have six monster ships building for her Navy. These are made up thus: Two battleships, be-

lieved to be of over 18,000 tons, voted in 1906;
one armoured cruiser of 16,000 tons, voted in
1906; two battleships of 18,700 tons, voted in
1907; one armoured cruiser of 19,200 tons,
voted in 1907.

England has seven monster ships building or
complete: the Dreadnought, voted in 1905, complete; the three 17,200-ton armoured cruisers
of the Invincible class, voted in 1905, completing; and three battleships of the Superb class,
and 18,600 tons, voted in 1906, building. In
addition, two battleships are to be voted under
the estimates of the present year, and a third
may be laid down if the Hague Conference fails
to secure disarmament. But these last vessels will not be laid down till the beginning of
1908.

Thanks to the enterprise of the London
Daily Express (see an article in that paper of
April 4th, 1907), we now know that the German
Admiralty has decided to turn the port of Emden, at the mouth of the river Ems, into a first-
class torpedo base. This decision is Germany's reply to the formation of the British
Home Fleet and the creation of a new flotilla
of torpedo-boat destroyers at Dover. Emden is
the nearest German harbour to the English

coast, and is some fifty miles nearer to Sheerness than Wilhelmshaven, which has hitherto been the most westerly of Germany's naval ports. It will be remembered that Emden is the port which is always chosen by novelists and story writers as the point at which the German army is embarked for the invasion of England. Embarkation wharves extend for over a mile along the right bank of the Ems, but apart from this the place is not very well adapted for the purpose usually allotted to it. The fortifications are very feeble, and there are only a few troops quartered there, while for many miles the line of railway leading up from the military centres is a single one.

These difficulties, however, could easily be surmounted, and they do not in the least affect the decision of the German Government. The principal German naval base in the North Sea is Wilhelmshaven, and this is connected with Emden by the Ems-Jahde Canal, about forty miles in length, which is deep enough to allow of the passage of small torpedo craft. By using this canal, whatever force of torpedo-boats is at Wilhelmshaven can reach Emden without touching the sea at all, and it is stated that it is extremely unlikely that a force of boats will

be permanently maintained at Emden. The
only craft to be there permanently will be the
necessary "mother ships." There is no doubt,
however, that the new base will provide a useful and dangerous striking point for Germany
should she ever come into conflict with Great
Britain.

The *Express* naval correspondent at Sheerness had an interview with an officer of the
Home Fleet at that port. "I am greatly surprised," he said, "that the move has not been
made before. Emden will certainly be of much
more use to Germany as a torpedo base than as
a possible jumping off place for an invasion
which in all probability they would never risk.
It brings their torpedo craft within eight hours
of the English coast."

"Do you think the British Admiralty will
have to make any answer to this step?" the
officer was asked.

"With the flotillas of destroyers now based
here and at Dover," he replied, "we ought to
be safe enough; but, in my opinion, the Sheerness flotilla spends far too much of its time in
the Channel and in the North of Scotland.
They call it the Nore flotilla, and it ought to be
the Nore flotilla, and nothing else. The divi-

sions at Sheerness and Dover should spend
most of their time cruising about off the mouth
of the Thames. The Home Fleet will be a fine
bait for these Emden torpedo craft, and we
cannot afford to run any risks of a surprise.''

Another officer whose opinion was asked
said:—''We cannot overrate the efficiency of
German torpedo vessels. If Emden is going
to be a torpedo base there ought to be at least
thirty-six destroyers at Sheerness, and twelve
continually at sea to prevent a surprise.''

Later reports brought the following information:—Between that port and Wilhelmshaven
runs the Ems-Jahde Canal, and whatever vessels of the size of German destroyers may be
at the dockyard port can reach Emden in less
than two hours, without touching the open sea
at all. The torpedo branch of the German
navy is the most efficient department of a very
efficient fleet. The men who man the craft are
all expert in their work, for they are entered
into the torpedo schools on joining the navy,
and never leave that branch until they quit the
service for good. The crews frequently receive lectures on the defences of British naval
bases. The full strength of the German navy
in torpedo-boat destroyers is seventy-one, and

as each ship is replaced as soon as it reaches
the age of ten years, they are in all respects
up to date. In the British Navy there are still
to be found several destroyers twelve, thirteen,
and even fourteen years old.

At present the German vessels, of which
forty-three are in full commission, are divided
between Wilhelmshaven, Cuxhaven (both North
Sea ports), and Kiel, and, as it is very improbable that any of those now in commission will
be reduced to the sham British standard of
"nucleus crews," the end of this year, when
the new harbour is completed, will see at least
forty modern and efficient German destroyers
within eight or nine hours' steaming distance
of the English coast.

As a protection against the possible attacks
of such a force, Great Britain maintains in the
North Sea only twenty-four fully-commis-
sioned destroyers, of which at the present five
are laid up for repair. Even when all of them
are fit for sea, they are frequently hundreds
of miles away in the English Channel or the
north of Scotland. Behind these ready-for-
war craft a considerable force of torpedo vessels is attached to the Nore Division of the
Home Fleet, but, as they are manned on the

pernicious nucleus crew system, they are practically negligible for immediate fighting purposes.   Besides, they are all assembled for ex-
ercises at Torbay, 340 miles from the North
Sea. The recent developments in German
naval organisation have no other object but to
threaten Great Britain's supremacy in those
waters which the creation of the Home Fleet
was intended to assert. That fleet came into
official existence on New Year's Day. So far,
its ready-for-war strength in the North Sea is
represented by two battleships to Germany's
sixteen. The Fifth Cruiser Squadron is still
existent only on paper.

In March, 1907, the *Rheinisch Westfaelische
Zeitung,* published at Essen, gave prominence
to a telegram from Berlin announcing on information derived from the best source that the
naval administration intends to purchase the
whole of the "Oberland" of Heligoland with
the object of fortifying the entire island.
Several tracts have already been bought, and
the garrison is now being reinforced by 420
men. It is proposed to turn the North Harbour
into a torpedo harbour for the active fleet, and
the harbour will be developed on a correspondingly large scale. The telegram continues:—

"The present fortifications are a half-measure, for they are unable to offer any effective resistance to the heavy turret guns of hostile warships, whose range, too, would out-distance the batteries of the island. The German people will understand why the plan has now assumed definite shape and development. Heligoland would be a plain hint to the Western Powers and an unmistakable reply to their recent machinations. Great Britain has ostentatiously increased her Home Fleet, and the new war harbour at Devonport is a fresh link in the chain of measures which stand in direct antithesis to the disarmament proposals which Great Britain is with suspicious zeal espousing. Let us make Heligoland a German Cronstadt which, covering the mouths of the Weser and Elbe and the Kiel Canal, together with the coastal defences on the mainland, will form a base within whose sphere an enemy will not lightly dare to intrude."

The *Berliner Neueste Nachrichten* states that it is only contemplated to improve the fortifications at a cost of £60,000. The German active battle fleet, or North Sea Squadron, consisted, middle of May, 1907, of the sixteen most up-to-date vessels in the Imperial Navy, with

two others in reserve at Wilhelmshaven. It
has now been decided to add two battleships
to the active fleet and two to the reserve, bringing the total up to twenty-two.

The numerical inferiority of the British
Fleet in home waters, to which attention has
so often been called of late, will be greatly increased by this augmentation of the German
fleet in service. The British Channel Fleet,
which covers the North Sea, contains fourteen
battleships in full commission; Germany will
shortly have eighteen in the same waters. In
the Home Fleet at the Nore there are six more
battleships, but these, as was admitted in the
House of Lords, are largely manned with un-
trained crews, and cannot be regarded as in-
stantly ready for war. The British total is
therefore twenty to the German twenty-two,
the percentage ready for immediate hostilities
being respectively 70 and 82. In addition, the
German torpedo flotilla is much stronger than
the British, and, unlike it, is always in the
North Sea and ready for instant service.

This change is typical of what has been going
on for the past three years (1904-1907).
While the British Naval Estimates have been
reduced by six millions sterling, the German

have increased by three millions. While British arsenals and dockyards are being reduced and neglected, those of Germany are being rapidly developed. It is only a continuity of policy on both sides that has led to the reduction of the number of British ships in full commission and an increase in the German.

GERMAN NAVY LEAGUE

In many ways even more important than all that has been done by the Germans in the matter of ship-building for purposes of war, is the constantly growing intense interest of the German nation in those naval preparations. The German Navy League is well known as the mouthpiece of the German Government. Here are a few facts about the activity of that League, brought down to May, 1907:—

During the last year the membership of the League increased from 865,000 to 906,000, whereas the British Navy League only numbers about 20,000 members.

The Navy League of German Women works in co-operation with the Navy League itself, and numbers many thousands of enthusiastic women friends of maritime expansion. During the last twelve months nearly 2,000 public

meetings were held under the auspices of the
League. Six hundred thousand copies of a
naval handbook were sold at cost price, and
500,000 copies of a pamphlet on "Germany's
Naval Power" were supplied to the branches
for distribution. The lectures and meetings
were supplemented by biograph productions
showing pictures of the fleet at sea and other
phases of naval life. One of the most important features of the work of the League was the
propaganda conducted among school teachers
and schoolboys at State schools. Many thousands of pamphlets and leaflets were distrib-
uted to teachers, who also received from the
League's officials much general information
about the navy, in writing.

Three hundred teachers from inland towns
were conducted on a four days' excursion to
Hamburg and Kiel, at the expense of the
League, to enable them to see the importance
of Germany's mercantile interests and the size
of the fleet with their own eyes. Several excursions of schoolboys to Kiel were also ar-
ranged at the expense of the League, which
thus enabled between 2,000 and 3,000 German
lads to obtain a personal interest in the Kaiser's fleet. Special railway excursions were

also run from many inland places to Kiel at low prices, to enable Germans in general to view the fleet. The monthly paper issued by the League has a circulation of 355,000. These particulars prove clearly enough that great popular interest and enthusiasm exist in Germany in regard to the navy.

Count von Reventlow, the well-known German naval expert, has given the *Daily Mail's* Berlin correspondent a statement of the reasons why limitation of naval armaments is rejected by the Kaiser's Government. He proposed as an inscription over the Conference Hall at the Hague, "Si vis bellum, para pacem" ("If you wish for war, prepare for peace").

Count von Reventlow argues that Germany must follow England's principle of maintaining a fleet able not only to guard her coasts, but to maintain unimpaired the over-sea communications vital to her existence. "In this region of national defence England has been the world's schoolmaster. We in Germany confess ourselves without exception believers in the English doctrine, for the soundness of which English history furnishes such brilliant confirmation. How far our teacher interprets the meaning of 'coast-defence' is apparent from her old strategic principle that in war one's own lines of defence must be laid on the enemy's shores.

"It lies, indeed, in the incompleteness of human nature that Christian altruism has not yet become the common possession of the nations. So must we Germans acknowledge that we still possess enough wicked egoism to defend our property to the maximum of our strength. As yet, Germany is far from having reached this point.

"It is obvious that many Englishmen should wish to see the cost of their Navy reduced. But here again Germans are so devoid of altruism that they cannot set the desires of English taxpayers above German life interests. I can only repeat my former proposal that England slacken her armaments until the completion of the German naval programme in 1920, when both fleets will be about equally strong. Then will the millennium be at hand, and taxpayers can sacrifice a cock to Æsculapius."

GERMANY IN THE MIDDLE EAST

The attentive reader of the preceding statements of fact cannot possibly think that German enterprise for purposes of greater national expansion is nothing more than a pious wish of a few professors or other academic people. This enterprise is distinctly imperialist; it is consciously the set resolution of a great nation to assert their place of prominence in the supreme council of nations. One has only to read what the Germans have recently commenced doing in far-off Persia, to get a very clear idea of their determined bid for imperial power of the first magnitude. In a valuable and authentic report published in the *London Daily Express*, of April 3, 1907, we read as follows:

"Germany, in need of new fields of expansion, has marked down Persia as a favourable country for exploitation, and elaborate plans have been worked out for the promotion of German commercial interests and the extension of German enterprise in the Shah's dominions.

"These plans are to be carried out by German capitalists supported by the German Government, in spite of the fact that every step forward contemplated by the Germans involves an invasion of the recognised sphere of British influence and an attack on British interests in Persia. German enterprise in Persia thus promises to bring about a critical situation in the Middle East, besides increasing the tension between Great Britain and Germany already existing in Europe.

"Germany's schemes for exploiting Persia are so menacing to British interests that they merit serious attention on the part of His Majesty's Government.

"Hitherto Great Britain and Russia have been the only Powers with extensive influence at Teheran. North Persia has been recognised as the Russian sphere of influence, and South Persia as the British. The Anglo-Russian agreement, now practically concluded, provides for the removal of future causes of rivalry in Persia.

"This arrangement between Great Britain and Russia is extremely distasteful to Germany, who desires to further her own ends in Persia. It is significant, however, that the commercial development now beginning is to be confined to South Persia, and carefully excluded from North Persia.

"In plain words, this means that the German Government is willing to patronise an invasion by German merchants of the British sphere of influence, while carefully avoiding any action that could give offence to Russia. German protestations of friendship for England cannot conceal the fact that the scheme now begun in Persia with the consent and knowledge of the German Government is an effort to gain a footing in a country adjacent to Britain's Indian Empire.

"The German Orient Bank was founded more than a year ago to promote profitable enterprises in Eastern countries. Its own capital amounts to £800,000, and its founders and backers are three of the most powerful institutions in Germany—the Dresdner Bank, the National Bank of Germany, and the Schaffhausen Banking Association. One of its directors, Herr Gutmann, junior, is now at Teheran to begin practical business operations in Persia.

"The plan of campaign has been carefully worked out, and begins with the establishment of a German bank at Teheran to compete with the British and Russian banks already there. The main object of this bank will be to secure concessions.

"The German Orient Bank will also try to establish a great commercial centre at the most favourable port on the Persian Gulf, obtaining a concession of territory as the site of the necessary buildings. This would be the headquarters of a new German line of coasting steamships to distribute to all the Persian ports the German exports brought to the chosen commercial centre by the Hamburg-America and other German lines.

"The steamships of the Hamburg-America Company now plying in the Persian Gulf undercut their British competitors by charging 8s. a ton of freight as compared with 12s. a ton rate of the British ships, and it is expected that a continuation of this policy will drive the British flag out of the Gulf.

"An audacious scheme of railway construction, seriously encroaching on British rights, completes the project of the German Orient Bank. It is stated that one of these projected German railways, running from Teheran to Bagdad, would earn profits simply by conveying the corpses of pious Persians to two holy places southward of Bagdad, where the Persian Moslems desire to be buried. Another projected railway, running from Bagdad eastward and then southward to the new German commercial centre on the Persian Gulf, would provide the urgently needed terminus for the Bagdad Railway.

"The German Government recently appointed a new Minister to Teheran, Herr Stemrich, an expert in Oriental affairs, to promote German commercial interests in Persia. One of Herr Stemrich's first acts was to recommend an immediate extension of German enterprise."

COMMERCIAL ENTERPRISE AND PROSPERITY

What makes all these far-reaching plans and preparations even more menacing, at any rate more important than they are at present, is this: that Germany, at home, is making such rapid strides towards an unprecedented progress of her national wealth and prosperity, that her oversea enterprises will, without doubt, easily find their necessary financial backing by capital in Germany. For this purpose, one has only to read the report of Mr. Consul H. Harris-Gastrell on the trade of the Kingdom of Wurtemberg, one of the South-German States, issued in 1907. In that country practically every industry is reported to be in a highly flourishing condition. Orders are pouring in, capital is doubling with unparalleled rapidity, wages are rising, and there is an extraordinary demand for labour. The British Consul says:—

"The general economic improvement in Germany . . . has continued steadily, and in the latter of the two years under review (1905-1906) attained a hitherto unprecedented height.

"There are no signs as yet of high-water mark having been reached, most manufacturers having orders for months in advance.

"The home labour supply has proved inadequate to meet the increased demands, and in some trades a considerable number of foreign workmen have been obtained.

"This scarcity of labour has resulted in a very general increase of wages, which in many industries amounts to more than a 10 per cent. rise, and also in many cases a shortening of the working day."

It is stated that the coal consumption of the German Empire has risen from 166,200,000 tons in 1904 to 195,000,000 tons in the first eleven months of 1906. Goods traffic on the railways on 1906 was double that of 1905.

The following table shows the amazing growth of German imports and exports during the past twelve years:—

IMPORTS

| 1894 | .. | .. | .. | £206,000,000 |
| 1906 | .. | .. | .. | £392,000,000 |

EXPORTS

| 1894 | .. | .. | .. | £166,000,000 |
| 1906 | .. | .. | .. | £306,000,000 |

An increase of nearly 100 per cent. in twelve years.

In most trades the only subject of complaint is the scarcity of workmen. The following are typical extracts:—

MACHINERY.—Employers complain of the difficulty of securing skilled technical labour.

MOTOR INDUSTRY.—The demand (in 1905-6) far exceeded the output.

BRICKMAKING.—The labour problem becomes more difficult every year. A large number of Italian workmen are now employed.

FURNITURE.—Manufacturers complain of the difficulty of obtaining skilled labour.

BOOT AND SHOE TRADE.—The industry has made good headway. The manufacturers complain of the difficulty in securing skilled hands.

One of the most striking evidences of Germany's amazing prosperity is given in the fol-

lowing remarkable statement of capital invested in industrial undertakings:—

Capital invested in the year 1904 £11,250,000
   ,,   ,,   ,,   1906 £19,500,000

An increase of nearly 75 per cent. in two
years.

IMPERIALISM: GERMAN AND BRITISH

The upshot, then, of a cool and sincere inves-
tigation into the state of German political,
naval and economic conditions is this: that the
Germans do think of expanding their country
into an empire proper, and that they have all
the means of doing so. They have the money
for it; they have, as was shown above, the
requisite prudence and the firm resolution to
avoid complications on the Continent; they are
fast getting the navy for the carrying out of
their imperialism. Now, unless a person is
ready to maintain that a man who is actually
in a position which entitles him to assume that
he can readily double his income, will yet and
in all cases, abstain from doing so; unless, we
say, one is inclined to assert such a thing, we
cannot possibly assume that the Germans will,

in the near future, abstain from further expansion, industrial and imperial. There have been single individuals who, like Sylla, quietly withdrew into private life, although all the treasures of power and wealth were in their hands. But there is in history no record of an entire nation that has ever done such a thing. We have no right whatever to presume that of the Germans. On the contrary, for the reasons given, we are obliged to expect them to proceed with ever greater energy on the road to imperialism, or to "world-power" as they call it.

In the opinion of the present writer, the inability of so many thousands of Englishmen to see aright in all questions of the relation of Germany to Great Britain is largely due to the ignorance in which they are about the real driving causes of their own, of British Imperialism. The average Briton lives and dies in the belief that the great achievement that we call The British Empire was made chiefly by a sort of innate genius of the "Anglo-Saxon Race." That blessed expression seems to account for everything. It is, in fact, not too much to say, that forty people out of fifty will conveniently account for most things under the sun by referring them either to the weather or to the

Anglo-Saxon Race. Yet, with due deference
to both of these remarkable Powers, it might
be urged with no mean lack of probability, that
there are quite a number of historical, political
and other events that can be traced back to
neither of the so-called four seasons in England, nor to the influence of the Anglo-Saxon
Race. British Imperialism is one of these
events. It was made neither by meteorolog-
ical, nor by racial qualities. It was made, because it had to be made; because Imperialism
was more necessary to the dwellers of Great
Britain than was either the Church of England
or the Temperance Movement.

British Imperialism began with William the
Conqueror, or the famous Franco-Norman who
succeeded the only one of all English Kings to
engrave the date of his greatest battle upon the
memory of every Englishman. This is now not
too far from 850 years. Imperialism in this
country is older than Oxford University, the
House of Commons, the Church of England, the
Nonconformist Churches, the English Sunday,
or the English language. At first that Imperialism spent itself in France (from 1066 to
1453), and then when it was found out that
France could not be conquered, it worked at the

incorporation of Ireland and Scotland, and when
that was finished (1707), it went abroad and
fought and wrought together the present British Empire. The same reason that made the
English of 1900 say, "from Cape to Cairo,"
made them say in 1100, "from the Tweed to
Biarritz," or (as Biarritz did not exist at that
time) "from Berwick to Bordeaux." It was
always the same thing. Imperialism is not a
matter of choice, or of Knight-errantry, a sort
of Don Quixote enterprise. This was partly
taught by the late Professor Seeley; but quite
wrongly. It was not by "absent-mindedness"
that the British Empire was founded. It was
an imperative necessity that called it into existence. We venture to refer our readers to our
book *Imperialism* (1905, Hutchinson) for further details.

Here we speak of these things only because
we mean to bring out as strongly as possible
the fundamental nature of all Imperialism
proper. This nature spells Necessity. The
Romans did not build up their Empire because
in a moment of bored leisure they said to themselves: "Life is a nuisance—let us go and do
something—suppose we conquer the world!"
They conquered the world because they were

placed before the alternative of perishing at once or conquering everything. Now, the Germans of our days are in a similar position. They are at present over sixty million people; that is, the German Empire already contains more European whites than does the British Empire. They are exceedingly prosperous, and, since wealth increases the greed for luxuries even more rapidly than the power to make money, the Germans are daily getting more and more anxious for the possession of new fields of commercial activity and power. But how can they do justice to these immensely powerful desires of theirs unless they expand into a world-empire? They must become a world-empire or they must abdicate.

THE GERMAN ABROAD

At a great number of "classes" or discussions after lectures and other public addresses, the author has heard it remarked by various British men and women, that if the Germans want to expand their commerce, they can very well do so without waging war with England, since England does not roll any obstacles whatever in the way of German immigration into British Colonies. This is as yet perfectly true.

Germans may at present leave their Fatherland, repair to, say Australia, and there establish any business of their own under conditions and circumstances identical with those applying to an Englishman. No discrimination is made against them. They may buy land, open shop, trade, import or export, teach, perform—in short, do anything they please, without anybody forcing them to become British citizens, or laying upon them any burden heavier than that laid upon British citizens.

All this is quite true; and if the Germans were still where they used to be in the first half of the nineteenth century; if their Fatherland was still a geographical expression rather than a high-strung national State, then, and then alone, we might very well expect them to emigrate without much heartburning or patriotic compunction. However, this has long since ceased to be the case. Germany is no longer a geographical or purely literary expression. It is an intensely developed national polity; a nation instinct with all the powers, pride, and passion of the older nations, such as the British and the French. Thousands of Britons could find comfortable berths in countries other than such as belong to the British Empire; say in

Russia, Hungary, Italy or Austria. Yet few
of them avail themselves of the opportunity,
simply because they do not care to live in a
country not their own. And if any British
journalist or statesman should publicly preach
emigration of Britons to non-British countries,
he would be regarded as an enemy of England.
It is even so in modern Germany. They do not
want to lose hundreds of thousands of their
compatriots to America or to the British Empire. They want to keep them. They want to
talk German, to make *Deutschthum and
Deutschland* one and the same thing. If, therefore, anybody should counsel them to unburden
themselves or the surplus of their teeming population in Australia or South Africa, they
would consider such a suggestion as a malig-
nant one, as a personal insult. Can we wonder
at that?

Is it not quite natural that a nation that has
by hard-won victories finally realised its secular dream of political unity does not feel inclined to encourage emigration into foreign
countries? The German, as is well known,
easily assimilates himself to new and stronger
nationalities. During a five years' stay in the
United States, we have never seen a German

who had remained German in his mode of thinking and feeling. One of them, Judge Stallo,
said he did; but he did not. We convinced ourselves of that by personal intercourse. The
Canadian French still retain their fine language of the times of Louis XIV.; the Germans
in the States drop the idiom of their original
home in less than one generation.

There is, be it remarked in passing, a peculiar reason for that. No ordinary German,
whose parents were folk living in small provincial towns in the country, talks "high" or book-
German. They all talk a dialect, and Germany
bristles with an incredible number of dialects,
jargons, modes of pronunciation, and so on.
To any one well acquainted with German, it is
the easiest thing in the world to tell the social
status of any given German man or woman by
the language he or she uses, and more especially by his or her pronunciation. Now, the
majority of German-Americans are the children of very humble German folk. Learning
German from their parents, they can talk only
such German as their parents gave them, that
is, peasant German. Rather than reveal, by
their pronunciation, that they come from peasant stock, the German-Americans pretend not

to know German at all, and even willingly forget their "Dutch," as they call it. In any case,
the Germans in the States, as everywhere else,
become first oblivious of, then indifferent to,
their original language, and so to thousands of
mental moods and attitudes ingrained in the
language. They   de-Germanize   themselves.
This is but too well known to the people of Germany. They dread emigration more than anything else. It institutes to them a national
danger, a loss in humans.

A very curious instance of this facile de-Ger-
manization of some Germans occurred a few
years ago in—Germany herself. When for
purposes of higher policy, a great number of
Polish families were transplanted from Prussian Poland to Westphalia, with its purely German population, it was soon found out that
many a German peasant, under the singular
spell of the Polish women, began to neglect his
own vernacular, and to talk Polish. This too
is not incomprehensible. The Germans have,
on the one hand, become very sensitive as to
their newly acquired national unity, and united
nationality; on the other hand, that feeling,
stronger in words than in fact, has not yet
reached the intensity and firmness that we find

in members of nations who, like the English or French, have each been nationally united for several hundred years.

Emigration, then, no matter what facilities may be offered to the Germans, is the very, method they disapprove of most. In fact, their leaders do everything in their power to fill their compatriots with a strong aversion from leaving Germany for a British or American country. If, moreover, we take into consideration the great and constantly rising prosperity of contemporary Germany; especially if we remember that what the German industrials lack most is human labour, as Count Posadowski, Imperial Home Secretary, has publicly remarked, and as was shown above in detail; we cannot but come to the conclusion that emigration to non-German countries is not a way out of the difficulty, because it is not likely to be resorted to by very many Germans.

But if emigration is discouraged and discredited, what else can the Germans do to satisfy their irresistible desire for expansion? Their own colonies are far and unprofitable, and not favourable in point of health. On the Continent, for reasons just given, they cannot expand otherwise than at the risk of a Euro-

pean coalition against them. What else *can*
they do? The average Briton has never given
that matter the slightest thought; and if he has,
he dismissed it with a vague smile. Or has the
author not repeatedly heard Englishmen say,
in effect, that if a war with Germany should
break out, it will be "not in our lifetime," but
"in a hundred years from now"? To one who
studies German preparations every day of his
life; to one who knows German and the Germans, their history and literature; to such a
person such remarks send a cold shiver through
his heart. After the awful experience of the
Boer War, to talk like that of a war with the
best-trained, highest-spirited, and most dangerous nation in the world! It is nothing short
of appalling.

IMPERIALISM AND THE BIRTH-RATE

Of course, there is still another way out of
the difficulty. It is one that implies no hardship whatever to the British, and is therefore
welcome to them. It is, moreover, a radical
solution of the whole German question. It
would leave no secret animosity against England in the hearts of the Germans. Undoubtedly there is such a method. It has long been

known to various nations. This method is—
to have but very few children; in other words,
to Malthusianise the nation. Why the Germans, in order to please the British and to rid
them of all bother about wars (a bother that
might interfere with British amusements at
music halls, racecourses, comedy theatres, and
other sublime places), why we say, the Germans
do not adopt this method of settling the whole
business, one cannot really quite see. It would
be so nice of them. However, they do not
adopt it. The wide and spacious German
women will persist in bringing forth such a
number of young Teutons that in the last forty
years they have outdistanced France by over
twenty million people. In fifty years from now
the Germans will certainly be a matter of far
over 100,000,000 people in the German Empire
alone. From the Kaiser downwards, they have
all numerous families. The fact is that the
Germans have quite appropriated the great lesson about the connection between Imperialism
and children. They know that a nation which
has reached a certain number must irretrievably
grow Imperialist, or otherwise—Malthusianise
herself. We take the liberty of here quoting
part of an article which we published in the

Daily Express of April 18, 1907, and in which
we gave a *résumé* of some of the ideas of our
book on *Imperialism* (1905).   We said:—

"It is well known that millions of modern
men and women are, as they think, 'dead
against all Imperialism.' It is to these and
their friends that I should like to submit some
human remarks on the relation of Imperialism
and children. For this purpose, we shall
shortly regard the modern history of France.
Repeatedly the French, or rather their rulers,
attempted to widen the territory of France in
Europe, that is, to found a French Empire.

"The last attempt, clearly prepared by the
Republicans of the great Revolution (1789-
1799), was realised, for a time, by Napoleon
I. He imperialized many a country round
France. However, the French nation, more
especially the French women, hated Napoleon's
imperial ideas. These women, all-powerful in
France, sapped and sapped the popularity of
Napoleon, whom they called the man-eater.

"When, therefore, Napoleon lost a battle or
two in 1813 and 1814, the French, instead of
rallying round their great Imperial leader, as
the Spanish had done round Palafox, Castanos,
or Cuesta, for over seven years, at once cooled

off, and Napoleon went first to Elba and then to St. Helena. The French had missed their chance of making an empire.

"Napoleon, the greatest political thinker of modern times, had clearly seen that the French, already in his time the most populous nation in Europe (even Russia was then less populous), imperatively needed more elbow-room for—children. Unless the French, Napoleon thought, get greater chances for human expansion, they will either emigrate, or—they will, given their national and secular passion for thrift, cease having children. This is precisely what happened. The very reason that made French women hate Napoleon, namely, that he sent so many Frenchmen out of France, makes them hate their large colonies. Madame does not want to leave France; and what Madame dislikes, the gods, being French and polite, do not approve of either. Hence, one thing alone remained. 'Let us adopt,' the madames said, 'the system of that amiable English clergyman, Malthus, and have as few children as possible.' This they have sedulously done ever since: with this interesting result, that France, in 1815 more, much more populous than Germany, is now 22,000,000 less populous than the empire of William II., although the areas of the two countries are practically the same.

"The human note, thus, comes to this: Napoleon's Imperialism, fiercely attacked by French and non-French Socialists, *pacifistes*, 'humanists,' positivists, anarchists, women, and professors of history; Napoleon's Imperialism cost the French some two million men, it is said. I know that this figure cannot be positively proved. But I accept it. Napoleon killed two million men for Imperial purposes. The Germans, too, lost a similar number. Well, may I learn, who killed the twenty-two million French now missing? One wonders. . . .

"Kill the Imperial sentiment, and you kill millions of babes. Kill the Imperial sentiment: loosen the Imperial ties; try to manœuvre out of it, to make silly compromises, or to dupe it somehow or other, and in the end you will have manœuvred your nation out of children, and duped your honour out of all shape."

The British reader—who is, we are afraid, too much given to a minimizing of any danger of invasion of or war with Great Britain— ought to ponder the preceding reflections with great care. The question really comes to this:

What *can* the Germans do but expand? And since they cannot possibly expand on the Continent, they must necessarily expand by sea-power, which inevitably means conflict with The Sea-Power of the world—with Great Britain. The one way out of the difficulty would be the artificial restriction of the fast-growing population of Germany. This the Germans do not want to resort to; and surely no Briton can, in common decency, advise or force them to do so.

WAR IS INEVITABLE

What, then, can be the ultimate upshot of all these circumstances? War—conflict; nothing else. The reader is most seriously requested to take all the preceding remarks and observations into consideration. We do not say that a given German, or this or that set of Germans, as such, hate the British. We positively know he or they do not. We are convinced by facts under our immediate observation that a very considerable portion of the Germans are rather favourably inclined towards the British. We know that untold numbers of them sincerely admire English literature, English ways and social manners. But

we do know, at the same time, that such sympa-
thy or admiration does not alter the crucial
point—that is, the fact that Germany wants
more expansive power at the expense of the
British. Between Germany and Great Britain
there is an antagonism that can be gotten over
only by means of armed conflict.

All through history we see such antagonisms.
There was the same antagonism between Athens
and Sparta; between Rome and Carthage; between the Greek and the Roman Catholic
Church; between England and France in the
Middle Ages and up to Waterloo; between the
North and the South of the United States; and
between many a minor set of nations. It has
nothing to do with personal likes or dislikes;
with the sayings of the Press; with dynastic
differences; or with "racial" views. It is in
the nature of things. It is like the conflict between day and night, between winter and summer, or between youth and old age. It can be
staved off for a time; it can never be averted
altogether. In the present work it is our object to make this as clear and convincing as
possible. For it needs a lot of convincing in
this country. In Germany every single person
is and has long since been sufficiently convinced.

In Germany every able-bodied man is a soldier. Together with his education as an efficient unit for military purposes, he is taught a little history, and the great spirit of an aggressive and growing nation is infused into him. In a country where practically every one man is or has been a soldier, the necessities of war are amongst the A B C of things; they are known to everybody. There is not a grown person in Germany but knows that, just as he individually has to obey his military superior in order to keep the whole of the German army in sound form, even so, all over Europe, each nation has to obey her superior, that is, the commands of European balance of power.

We do not ignore that many an Englishman fondly imagines that Socialism in Germany is a disruptive force, or one that will impede or incapacitate Germany in any attempt at making political moves of European grandeur. No greater illusion can possibly be indulged in. Socialism in Germany, as everywhere else on the Continent, except France, is a purely theoretic force. It yields to the first onslaught of any one of the old historical and real forces on the Continent. Witness the signal defeat of Socialism in the recent (1907) elections in Germany, when the Kaiser and his councillors advanced the real forces of their political army. Socialism in Germany is politically not a party based on historic realities, but only a manœuvre based on abstract ideas of a certain school of economists. Now, if there is one thing more certain than another, it is this: abstract theories cannot, in the long run, undo historic and practical forces.

In England, these two hundred years, there have been any number of "parties" teaching abstract novelties, such as Theism, Atheism, Positivism, and so on. They have never been able to cope with the historic and practical force called the Anglican Church. It is even so with Socialism in Germany. It is abstract. It was called into existence by two scholars, by Karl Marx and Ferdinand Lassalle. The very fact that both were originally of Jewish extraction, that is, that neither had had a share in the real life of the historic forces of Germany, shows that Socialism is born of abstract ideas. It can cause, and it has caused, much disturbance and discussion; it cannot build up or destroy Germany. Bismarck, faithfully continuing the traditions of the old and historic class of *Junker*, or country squires, to which he belonged; Bismarck, we say, did build up the unity of Germany, and Lassalle failed.

A nation is not a piece of mineral on and with which one can make any experiment one chooses. A nation is something organic, and refuses to be handled by abstract and mechanical measures. They, therefore, who indulge in any thought of Germany being seriously crippled or thwarted by her Socialists are living in a fool's paradise. Has not Bebel, the acknowledged leader of the German Socialists, repeatedly declared that his party does not believe in disarmament, in settling all international disputes by the Hague Tribunal, and also that he and his will unhesitatingly take up arms in defence of Germany, or in any cause involving the honour and greatness of the Fatherland? Bebel has drawn upon himself the severe strictures of M. Hervé, the anti-militarist leader of the French Socialists, but he did not mind that very much.

Germany has parties—even a peace party. However, those parties are like mere shadows, as compared with the real power in Germany—the State, *i.e.*, principally Prussia. The average Englishman has not the least idea of the extent to which, in Germany, the influence and

interference of the State has practically nulli-
fied all other activities in the public or political
life of the German nation. The nearest example in England to that effect are the great banks
in England. A bank such as the London and
South-Western Bank, or the London and County
Bank, may have and does have more than a
hundred branch offices each; but everybody
knows that all the business of those banks is
decided and managed at headquarters. The
local managers have no power worth speaking
of. It is all done at the central office. This is
what happens in Germany with the whole public and political life of Prussia or Bavaria sev-
erally. In such a country, as one may readily
gather, political parties have very little to say;
and Government always finds means to play
out any party by dexterous electioneering
moves. Under these conditions the Socialists
in Germany, anyhow hateful to Government,
can be and have actually been played out by
adroit managing of the elections. The Socialists, then, have no power to stop or retard the
aggressiveness of the German State.

Other extreme lovers of peace in this country indulge in another set of day-dreams. They
think, and even say in public, that the Ger-

mans do not in the least mean to be aggressive to Great Britain, and that the war fleet they are building is merely a defensive fleet, that is to say, one for the legitimate defence of the growing and considerable maritime interests of the Germans. Now, as half-truths are, as a rule, more dangerous than a full-fledged untruth, it may be said that the foregoing statement is one of pernicious half-truth. Nobody means to deny that the maritime commerce and the oversea interests of the Germans have in the last thirty years been increasing at a very rapid rate. Nobody, therefore, can deny the Germans the right of seeing to the protection of their vast trade by means of a big fleet of men-of-war. Yet it is equally true that the idea that the principal object of the German fleet is defensive and not aggressive is thoroughly and hopelessly wrong and absurd.

A merely defensive army is a military nonentity. The British naval victories were all won hundreds and thousands of miles away from England—at Copenhagen, at Cape St. Vincent, at Lagos, Trafalgar, Abukir Bay, etc. That means, the English did not think of matters naval what now so many British think of matters military. They always believed in offen-

sive warfare; they attacked the enemy outside
the English Channel or the German Sea—in the
Atlantic, in the Mediterranean, and elsewhere.
They were, in order to be efficiently defensive,
in the first place effectively offensive. This is
an old, old principle of all warfare; and of all
the nations, the Germans are fully and clearly
aware of it. They do not for a moment believe
that their fleet is meant only for purely defensive purposes. They know that such a statement is absurd and impossible. They know
that to be really able to defend the German
trade anywhere, they must be in a position to
attack any one of their rivals or enemies in any
sea. If, therefore, the German fleet is said to
be one for defensive purposes only, it is, when
uttered by Germans, a downright hypocrisy;
when by British persons, an unmitigated folly.
The German fleet can have and has only one
possible aim—that of attack, of offensive warfare, just as has the German army, and even
very much more so. The German army is
checkmated to a large extent by a possible coalition of the rest of the Continental armies. The
German fleet is not thwarted by such a coalition
of sea-Powers.

As the reader may see, it is here contended

that the ultimate and even the proximate intention underlying all the moves of the German Empire and the Kaiser is quite patent. There is no doubt about it. It is, of course, true that if one tries to read the real mind of the Germans from hundreds of occasional or chance remarks, articles, or other utterances of theirs, then indeed the task of making a concordance of the bewildering and contradictory statements of the German Press—official and non-official— becomes overwhelming. However, in a problem as great as is the near conflict between Germany and England, it does not matter very much what this paper or that statesman says or does not say. William Pitt, shortly before the outbreak of the endless wars with France from 1792 to 1815, publicly declared that Europe was going to have a period of complete peace lasting at least fifteen years. If one now reads the *Times* or the *Globe* of a hundred years ago, one is amazed beyond words at the profound ignorance in which the writers of these papers were with regard to the near future of Napoleon or the Continent. The German question is, like all great questions, almost independent of this or the other chance thing or event. In European history there always have been currents of events, just as in the sea there are currents of water. And, just as no whale or shark can stem or alter the gulf-stream, even so no ruler or diplomatist can deflect certain historic currents in Europe. To this, as to a very important element of our study of the German question, we shall soon return.

BRITISH MYOPIA

At present we want to dwell a little upon the effect of the opposite view. We mean the view that the German question is not clear at all; that we cannot as yet know what the Germans are after; and that the conflicting evidence to be gathered from an observation of the Germans is not sufficient to give us the desired clearness. Such views are spread even by papers of otherwise great value. It is precisely this view, which we combat, that has only lately (May 20) been put forward in an able leader in the *Morning Post*. We consider it our duty to show the inadequacy of such views. For this purpose we here append the leader *in toto*. It says:—

"The business of a statesman, said Bismarck a good many years ago, is to see things as

they are. What is the statesman's business is
also the business of every citizen in so far as
he concerns himself with his country's affairs
or with its relations with other countries. We
all want to see things as they are. Yet it is
not always easy. What, for instance, is at
present the idea and the feeling of the majority
of Germans on the subject of this country and
of British policy? If we were to be guided in
our judgment by what we read in some of the
German newspapers, we might imagine that the
Germans were all filled with apprehensions of
some dire design supposed to be cherished in
this country against the welfare, the expansion,
or even the peace of Germany. As no Englishman is aware of any such design; indeed,
as all of us know that no such design exists,
there would be a temptation to suppose the
population of Germany afflicted with some mental disease or with one of those extraordinary
delusions of which a once-much-read writer
wrote a history. But those who have in late
years travelled in Germany and mixed with the
people in that country have discovered that
among the educated class there the representative character of the newspapers is denied, and
it is asserted that the articles unfriendly to

England are not the expression of the popular feeling, or, at any rate, are not to be taken too seriously. Between those papers which make it their business to preach down England and those cultivated Germans who denounce these newspapers it is hard to get at the facts and see things as they are. The Germans outside of Germany, the travelled Germans, are not anti-British. They generally know something of England and the English. But they are not always listened to with respect by the Germans at home, at any rate not by all the newspaper writers. It is to be hoped that there will shortly be a change of fashion in Germany, and that the habit of discussing the imagined deep-laid plots of England will die out. Meantime it may help towards the clear view which is so desirable, to consider some of the undoubted facts about the German Empire which are apt to be forgotten, not only here, but there.

"Germany has for a whole generation been enjoying steady and increasing prosperity. None of the great States of Europe has so much to show in the way of material progress. Most of the large towns have been within the last twenty-five years so transformed as to seem to have been almost entirely re-built. The standard of comfort, and even of luxury, attained is beyond the dreams of the last generation. Manufacture, trade, and commerce have flourished exceedingly. The whole country bears on its face the marks of accumulating wealth. For education of all sorts and for the advancement and diffusion of knowledge provision is made on an ampler scale than in any other country of Europe. These great advances have followed close upon and seemed to be the consequences of the great struggles which led to the foundation of the new Empire as the form and symbol of national unity. Accordingly the national self-consciousness has been exalted, and Germans to-day take a legitimate pride in their country. The Army is considered, probably rightly, to be the best organised and best trained in the world, and the Navy has for a whole generation worked hard to make itself the Army's counterpart. Germany's influence makes itself felt far and wide, not merely in Europe. These are some of the marks of greatness in a nation. The nation that is so well situated in regard to its arrangements for defence, for education, and for trade, and of which the prosperity is so remarkable, can hardly have good reason to be excessively timid or anxious as to the future.

"Yet there are a number of writers in Germany who seem to spend their time looking abroad for possible troubles, and for several years past they have represented England as the most probable source of danger to Germany. If these writers had all been silent it is quite possible that traders and manufacturers in England and in Germany would have been conscious of a certain rivalry. Mr. Haldane, in a speech the other day, spoke of the 'legitimate antagonism of trade competition.' But it is by no means clear that this antagonism need have a national or international aspect. Two spinners in Bolton are much keener rivals one of the other than either of them of any German competitor, and yet they can manage to live together in the same town without quarrelling. It would not be easy to find a British trader or manufacturer who would wish this country to pick a quarrel with Germany. Some of them would be glad to be helped against German competition by a protective tariff, but they would not on that account wish the two nations to enter into the extreme competition of a war.

Moreover, men of business best realise that the best customers are rich, industrious nations, and that Germany and England, with or without tariffs on one side or on both, are necessarily bound to have very large commercial dealings with one another. Apart from manufacture and trade where the two nations are competitors, but not necessarily unfriendly competitors, what are the interests of the two nations which clash? We have never been able to discover them. There is no rational cause for a quarrel between England and Germany, and if a quarrel arises it must be due to some wrong, malice, or misunderstanding. These things it is not always possible to prevent. They ought not to arise, and it is the duty of each nation and of each Government to avoid being the author of any such occasion of dispute, and, of course, also to be strong enough in case of a gratuitous quarrel thrust upon it to defend itself.

"The latest misunderstanding, if it is a misunderstanding, seems to be due to the fact that King Edward, like the German Emperor, occasionally travels to visit the Sovereigns of other countries, and that these visits, on the whole,

have contributed towards closer relations between Great Britain and the other countries.
The wider the circle of these international cour-
tesies and kindnesses extends, the more likely
is the preservation of peace. That this view
should not commend itself to some of the German critics is remarkable seeing that Germany's great achievement is held to have been
the preservation of the peace of Europe by a
series of alliances. The close understandings,
first between the three Emperors and afterwards between Germany, Austria, and Italy,
are held by German statesmen to have been the
foundations of a European equilibrium that has
lasted some thirty years. A close understanding between England and France, between England and Italy, and between England and any
other Great Power is not likely to aim at any
disturbance of the *status quo* or at any attack
on other Powers. If, therefore, there are
alarms in Germany, the observer who wishes
to see things as they are must infer that they
are of purely German origin, and are not at-
tributable to any action that has taken place
outside that country. The problem which the
observer has to solve is to account for this

spontaneous generation of heat in a body politic having so many of the elements of health and strength as the German Empire."

The writer of the preceding article is quite right in his main contention, to the effect that, unless we can see things as they are, all our efforts to construe aright the political situation will be abortive. The present work is only an attempt to see things as they are, and as they will be on the basis of what they are at present (1907). In using the word "things," we mean to distinguish things from persons. In all politics, persons are of great importance; but in some questions of great or international politics, single persons are not all-decisive.

This is where the ordinary diplomatist or statesman makes his gravest errors. For instance, a given ambassador of Great Britain at the Court of Berlin is, by the very nature of his office, thrown in daily contact with the Kaiser, his Ministers, his other officials, and the various persons moving on the political stage of Berlin. These he, the ambassador, may and frequently does know very well. Seeing that these persons apparently do the whole of German policy, or that all the acts and documents coming officially from Germany may, at

least outwardly, be traced to the activity or influence of these persons—the ambassador, not
unnaturally, believes that they are the true
originators and, as it were, the causes of all
those documents and acts. And since the ambassador knows each of them intimately, he
readily persuades himself that he has a real
insight into their characters and minds, and
thus also into the real causes of German policy. However, in thinking so, that ambassador frequently, and in great international questions always, commits a fatal error.

The ultimate and true cause of events and
measures in German policy is not exclusively
in the characters and minds of a number of official persons in Berlin. In such great questions
there are impersonal causes driving on both the
non-officials and the officials. To these great
questions belongs, in the first place, the conflict
between Germany and Great Britain. It is a
conflict based on facts and tendencies independent of the will or belief of this or that individual man. It is in the very nature of things.
If, therefore, we continue to consult the sayings or doings of German official persons only,
or, for the matter of that, of British officials
only, we are not likely at all to get at the root

and driving cause of the whole question. Those sayings and doings may very well be contradictory, and are mostly misleading. They are meant to be so. This is also in the nature of things.

Again, is it not about high time that every man in this country should clearly understand a fact taught and observed by all unprejudiced students of European politics? We mean the fact that in all international matters the nations of Europe stand to one another nearly always in a "state of nature." They recognise but too frequently nothing but the law of Might, or the law of the stronger fist. However polished, "civilised," or "educated" the nations of Europe may be inside their respective boundaries and towards members of their own country, it is historically certain that in all very serious international questions they have almost invariably behaved like egoistic savages. One nation, in these matters, is as bad as another. Under these circumstances, we cannot allow ourselves to slip into the convenient belief that there will be no conflict with Germany, because this or that German minister or chancellor is "such a nice fellow." So he may be—in private life. As soon as he enters on life inter-

national, he is at once "in a state of nature."
From a German filled with the humanitarian
ideals of Lessing, Schiller, and Goethe, he becomes forthwith a human animal. As such he
obeys only the instincts of his uncontrolled nature, and all that he asks of his cultured intellect is to serve him with specious excuses for
his animal instincts. This, the good intellect
(read: lawyers, statesmen, journalists) always
furnishes him with.

Undoubtedly the Germans will, in case of
actual conflict, declare that they have been "out-
raged," "bullied," or "deceived" into it by the
"perfidious British." That goes without saying. The English have always been "perfidious." They won the battles of Crécy, Poitiers,
Agincourt, the victory over the Armada, the
battles of Naseby, the Boyne river, Cape La
Hougue, Blenheim, Malplaquet, Quebec, Plas-
sey, Wandewash, St. Vincent, Camperdown, the
Nile, and Trafalgar—all by "perfidy." They
made The Parliament—by "perfidy." They
persuaded Shakespeare to pose as the author
of *Hamlet* and a few other dramas, not unknown
to fame, written by some other person, probably a Prussian—by "perfidy." It has long
been proved. It cannot be doubted. In fact,

all great States are perfidious, and all small
ones are painfully honest. The Prussians, of
whom Prince Bismarck himself said that they
"made no moral conquests," the Prussians are
God-fearing goodies, or what our girls would
call "such dears."

If the thing was not so terribly serious, it
would be killingly funny. The average man
invariably takes the symptom for the cause,
the person for the thing, the skin for the bone,
and the occasion for the motive. In the present case we venture to submit that the matter
is so grave that it ought, for once, to persuade
even the average man of this country to pierce
the shell of things, and to grasp the core thereof.
We said above that in all European history
there are currents, "streams" of events which
cannot be unmade by the influence of any individual or any set of individuals. One of these
maelstroms is the antagonism between Germany and Great Britain. This, and this alone,
is the truth. All diplomatic incidents, such as
messages, speeches, press articles, conventions,
meetings, banquets, wires, and wireless reports,
are mere externals. They cannot alter the
stream. They may retard it; they may discol-
our it. They will never deflect it.

FOREWARNED IS FOREARMED

What, then, is the only thing to be done?
Evidently only one thing: prepare for the conflict. The Germans have learnt this lesson thoroughly. They are, as a nation and as individuals, preparing themselves carefully. Their
"Navy League" numbers close on a million
members. The British Navy League does not
exceed 20,000. In Germany every ablebodied
person is a soldier, filled with the great military
spirit—the spirit that made old Blücher say to a
tottering Prussian regiment in battle: "Ye
scoundrels, do you then want to live for ever?"
The spirit that prompts every German to think
that if he were not ready to die for his country,
what on earth is he living for?   The spirit that
shrinks from no sacrifice, from no self-denial,
from no hardship of discipline. The spirit that
is aware that to speak constantly of the rights
of citizenship is only half the thing; the more
important part is to think of the duties of citizenship. The spirit that fills a man with the
true sense of immortality, that is, with the feeling that he has obligations not only towards his
contemporary fellow citizens, but also to those

that will be his fellow citizens in the generation
to come.

This spirit is strength, great strength. It is
this spirit that has made our incomparable Europe, as thousands of years ago it raised the
Greeks, Jews, and Romans above all the other
nations of the world. That spirit can be combated only by a like spirit. Numbers will not
do. Spirit is vanquished by spirit alone. The
"two-power standard" is a mere snare. It is
the view of a grocer or a haberdasher. Now,
a grocer or haberdasher is a very valuable member of the community in his way; and the social
displacement from which he suffers in this country is most unjustified and absurd. But his
views on international questions are somewhat
narrow. He is apt to assume that, if a man
with £100 in his till has more business power
than the man with only £50 in his box, even so
a nation with two ships against one of its enemy
has the greater military power of the two.
Nothing can be more misleading. England beat
Spain, although the Armada consisted of very
many more vessels than were then in the possession of the English. The French beat all the
European armies, including British corps too,
from 1792 to 1813. The Japanese beat bulky

Russia; and the Boers held out close on three years against overwhelming odds. History is full of such examples; and, if people only cared to study it, they would find that all history is one of minorities. Look at a map of Europe. Russia is by far the largest territory; has she ever been the most important? England looks tiny enough on the map, as against Scandinavia, France, Spain, Germany, Austria-Hungary, Russia; has she not in the last two hundred years played first fiddle at more than one moment critical for all Europe?

To weigh probable success by numbers, to leave out the immense leverage of spirit, is not only ridiculous, but most dangerous too. Even in business, any observer who cares to study the question will find that, as a rule, he who begins on nothing, or with no capital to speak of, very frequently beats the heir or successor who commenced business with an established house and much capital. The former, the successful business man who had nothing at the start, had the right spirit; the other had not. The spirit, the great spirit is, we repeat it, the great winner of battles. There is no doubt whatever that the Germans at present are brimful with that spirit. They overdo it, no doubt; they are positively

swelled-headed; they suffer from *megalomania*.
Yet the very exaggeration of the thing proves
that the thing itself is there. And since such a
spirit can be combated only by a like spirit, the
question, the great and ominous question, arises
—whether this country has the same spirit.
Whether Great Britain and her people are ani-
mated by the same consciousness of the critical
situation of all Europe, which the Germans are
clearly aware of. Whether the average Briton
feels that Europe has come to a period of far-
reaching decisions. Whether he has any idea
at all that Europe, instead of having been all
during the last century a complicated game of
chess between six Great Powers, has now been
reduced to a simple duel between two Great
Powers only. Whether he can really grasp all
that this undeniable fact implies. Whether he
feels within himself the force to arouse himself
out of the slumber of self-complacency, and face
the stern tasks imposed upon him by history,
with a manly courage.

A Briton of to-day is not the son of his parents only. Two thousand years of history
weigh upon him. Two thousand years of
struggle, work, and extraordinary efforts—
mental, moral, and material—have laid upon

him an immense responsibility. He is not a
gentleman of independent means; he is a depositary. He must not think—and woe to him
and his nation if he does so think—that he can
draw on his means given him by sixty generations of heroes and workers, freely and *ad lib.*
He is a depositary; he will have to account for
his means to the next generation, and, unless
he be more careful than he is, to himself too.
Otherwise it will happen to him, what always
happens to faithless depositaries. He will lose
his honour, together with his means. Again we
ask, are we entitled to say that the average man
in this country is fully conscious of all these
momentous truths?

To say with childish self-complacency, "Our
fleet cannot be beaten" is too dangerous for
words. In history the Impossible alone is impossible. *Il ne faut jamais dire, jamais,* as
Prince Metternich used to say. If indeed, a
nation, well protected by Nature, trained
through secular practice and tradition is in
actual possession of a great naval force; and *if*
such a nation continues to do everything to keep
up her great efficiency; then, and only then, that
nation may with fair probability assume that
it cannot easily be beaten. But this constant

preparation requires two things before anything else: First, the right spirit in the whole
nation; and then, in addition to daily practice
in the art of war, a very careful study of naval
warfare in the past.

The spirit; the spirit—there is the whole matter. The spirit of earnestness, of real seriousness. The British are grave enough; are they
also sufficiently serious? Are they anxious
concerning the vast problems still to be solved
by them? They devote millions in money and
billions in words, written and spoken, to the
problem of the alleged intemperance of the
British nation. Do they devote adequate attention to the political intemperance of their
great rivals, the Germans? The very people in
Great Britain who go about preaching, writing,
lecturing, collecting money, etc., etc., to combat
the supposed intemperance of the British nation
—that can be easily proved to drink less than
one-third of the quantity of wine, beer, or
liqueurs consumed either in France, Germany,
or Austria-Hungary—the very people, we
say, go about preaching, lecturing, and writing
on the moderation and friendliness of a nation
that thinks of nothing, and can think of noth-

ing else than the destruction of British supremacy on sea.

Who does not know that the numerous goody-
goody "peace-at-all-price" people, who publicly
declare that Germany does not dream of attacking England, are mostly the very faddists
who tell and spread the grossly exaggerated
reports about the perdition of this country by
the consumption of too much drink? The various "peace societies" venture to say and publicly to state that Germany does not dream of
attacking England. And such criminal drivel
is said in the face of the fact that the Boers,
with only 50,000 men, against the 5,000,000 of
the Germans, did dare to attack British possessions a few years ago. Many people in England imagine that the Germans mean to invade
this country, even to possess themselves of it.
Nothing is more remote from the minds of the
Germans. At any rate, this is not at all the
principal idea. What they do think of, and
what in their international and home situation
they are bound to think of, is to win the supremacy on sea, or, if that be impossible, equality
on sea with the British. Invasion of England
is a mere incident in their plan. Once they de-

feat the British Navy in the North Sea; once
they hold this sea, as the Dutch repeatedly, and
for long periods, held it, they have attained
everything they really want.

The game of interests, counter-interests, side-
interests, and side-counter-interests amongst
the Powers of Europe is so subtle that no great
player of the game need despair of doing again
what has been repeatedly done before. The
Germans, we repeat it, do not contemplate an
invasion of this country; certainly not in the
first place. They saw, even in their successful
war with the French, that the second part of
that war, or the one in which the French nation
as such defended her territory, was by far less
successful than the first, where the Germans
fought the regular armies of France. The
great surrenders of whole corps happened in
the first part of the war only. The Germans
only meditate how to make it impossible for the
British to maintain the claim to supremacy on
sea. To this one great task the Germans sub-
ordinate all and everything. It dictates their
diplomacy, their acts, their preparations.

He who has never made a serious study of
History, is very likely to estimate wrongly many
a feature in the life of a nation. Thus, to give

just one instance, the so-called absurd movements in Society or in political life are almost
invariably misjudged by men unversed in the
study of the play of historic forces. Take as
an example the excessive theories now launched
in the sea of German literature. We have
heard of some of them in the previous part of
the present book. The average man laughs at
them, condemns them as unreasonable, and
thinks that, being unreasonable and absurd,
they must needs fail of success. No graver
error could be indulged in. Of two sets of social or political moves, the more absurd one has
by far the greater likelihood of success. Far
from pooh-poohing and contemptuously ignor-
ing these "absurdities," caused in Germany
by the overweening conceit of the German
teachers, leaders of thought, and their pupils,
we ought to take them into very serious consideration. A nation like the Germans, that
eagerly assimilates such theoretic stuff, is soon
ready to crave for the deeds crystallising those
theories in practical reality. In fact, had History been taught properly, no man in Great
Britain could for a moment doubt that the very
excesses and absurdities at present rife all over
Germany with regard to the immense *rôle* that

the Germans are "evidently" destined to play in the sublunar world, clearly indicate and prove that from mere vague hopes and dreams, the Germans are on the point of coming to deeds. Where there is so much smoke, flames are sure to break out soon.

GERMAN ASSETS

Leaving such general reflections, which, as we know, have not much weight with British readers, we hasten to point out some more concrete and palpable factors in the coming wave of German Imperialism. The Germans have various features of their own that distinguish them from former nations who attempted to build up great Empires. Thus, to speak in the first place, of one of the most important points: Nearly all previous nations showed a marked tendency to the artificial restriction of the growth of population, as soon as they passed the line of moderate wealth and reached the state of inordinate material prosperity. The ancient Romans, the richer they grew in money, the poorer they became in children. It was even so with the Greeks, the Byzantines, the Italian Republics, and many a modern state. Not so the Germans. Although their material prosperity has, in the last generation, risen by leaps and bounds almost unparalleled in modern times, their population, far from decreasing, is rising so quickly that, according to Schmoller, they will be 104,000,000 in the year 1965; according to Hübbe-Schleiden, 150,000,000 in the year 1980; and according to Leroy-Beaulieu, 200,000,000 in the year 2000.

At any rate, it is certain that as amongst the more advanced nations of Europe the Germans are now the most numerous by far, so they are likely to remain the most populous highly civilised nation in Europe. This is, one need hardly insist, a very important factor. They mean to expand imperially, and are fully convinced of their ability to do so.

Equally important is another feature of modern Germany. It consists in that the Germans, quite unlike the French, attained their utmost power, not through violent and destructive revolutions at home, but by means of a great and victorious war with the French outside Germany. The French obtained the greatest momentum of strength and power by and through a fearful civil convulsion attacking every one of the organs of their body-politic, by the French Revolution. Such convulsions

may and do give the nation so convulsed an
energy of the most intense kind, and hence an
unusual leverage in the conflict with other nations; yet the leverage acquired by the Germans, if not quite as great as that of France in
1794 or 1796, was made good without any fundamental upheaval of the whole structure of the
German polity. Consequently the Germans
show a steadier and surer growth in power.
Having grown steadily, they gained in sureness
of power what they lost in time and intensity.

The above two features are only part of a
series of distinctive advantages possessed by
Germany in the competition for rule and expansion. When, in former ages, the French were
the mightiest nation on the Continent, they yet
never counted amongst their advantages the
asset that Germany to-day is quite sure of.
France had allies, but they were, as a rule,
small Powers. Germany has a staunch and re-
liable ally that is not a small Power, Austria-
Hungary. France was never sure of either her
flanks or her rear. Germany is quite sure of
her rear. Finally, and perhaps principally, the
great efforts made by France to realise imperial expansion were much less the wish and ear-
nest desire of the French people than the dynas-

tic policy of her rulers. In Germany, at present, the people itself wants, believes in, and demands imperial expansion. In Germany an imperialist, like Mazarin in France, will not be hampered by dissensions at home, such as the Frondes of 1648-1653, which exasperated the great Cardinal.

All these undoubted facts conspire to make the situation of Germany a very strong one. To overlook them would be fatal to Great Britain. From her very situation in historic space, Great Britain has, ever since the Tudors, been one of the umpires of the Balance of Power in Europe. It matters everything to the British, whether the central State on the Continent, *i.e.,* Germany, is strong or weak, aggressive or submissive. Evidently, no State can eventually upset the balance of Europe as readily as can the central State. Napoleon I. himself became a European power only after he had practically seized most of Germany. He never had the whole of Italy, or of Spain; nor did it much matter. But the possession of Germany gave him the command of the Continent. Even of Austria-Hungary he never possessed as much as of Germany, although he defeated the Austrian armies more frequently. The greater half of the then Austrian monarchy, or Hungary, he never controlled. Yet he was the controlling Power on the Continent, because he practically controlled the whole of Germany. It is by such considerations that one may arrive at the true estimation of the fact, that there is now in the very centre of the Continent a strong and united Empire; the German Empire. The possibilities implied in this fact are boundless. So far any serious student of European politics must go with the most extreme of Germans. In fact, it must be admitted that no State in Europe is in a position so favourable for imperial expansion as is Germany. The more clearly we see that, the more fully we convince ourselves of the truth and force of this statement, the surer will be our step on the slippery ground of political conjectures.

GERMANY'S WEAK POINTS

In the preceding remarks we dwelt, and intentionally, on the strong and advantageous features of Germany as an international Power. It would be childish to deny that Germany suffers also from the defects of her virtues. She too has her weak points, her very faulty sides, and before coming to the final summing-up of

the facts and to the verdict, it is necessary to
dwell on some of the graver shortcomings inher-
ent in the German nation and empire. We are
going to do so at once. However, we cannot
omit remarking that before examining the
strong or the weak points of Germany, a Briton
ought never to lose sight of one cardinal fact
that is more than likely to render his view of
German politics unsafe.

Professor Schiemann, the well-known German politician and personal adviser of the
Kaiser, rightly said *à propos* of the late visit
of British journalists in Germany, that to the
average Briton Germany is quite unknown. To
this we add that, not only is this the case with
regard to present or contemporary Germany,
but still more so with regard to Germany in the
past, or to the history of Germany. Thus history might be left out from practical politics if
it did not shape it, if it did not influence it.
But it does. No one can understand contemporary German politics who does not possess
sound knowledge of German history. In English historical literature there are exceedingly
few authoritative books on German history.
While the Germans have written up every aspect of English history in a very large number

of elaborate, if not perfect books, the British have done, comparatively, very little with regard to German history. But even this does not show the full strength of the point we want to raise. Not only have the British no scholarly or practical knowledge of Germany, whether in the past or in the present, but they are also very likely to misconstrue the facts they do know on that subject.

Ever since the Middle Ages, the principal European enemies of England were the Dutch, the Spanish, and especially the French. In fact, from 1688 to the end of the nineteenth century, France was *the* hereditary enemy of England, or was considered to be so. In the course of the secular conflicts with France, the British naturally learned much about the temper, habits, tendencies, and resources of the French. As in all wars we want to adapt ourselves to the means of our adversary, one may state with absolute accuracy that the British diplomatic, naval and also partly the military traditions are distinctly adapted to and meant to serve in conflicts with a particular sort of enemy, with the French. Undoubtedly, many a British diplomatist or admiral, saturated with the secular traditions of Anglo-French wars, would be a match for any French diplomatist or admiral. Nothing is more likely. It is, however, still doubtful whether that British diplomatist would prove as efficient a representative in diplomatic conflict with Germany too.

We have only to consult history to find, that, for instance, James I. committed a long series of blunders because he persisted in treating Spain as if she had been what France then really was. He knew France, so he simply applied his method of dealing with France to his way of dealing with Spain. It can hardly be doubted that, in all diplomatic, naval, or military conflicts with Germany, means other than those that applied to France must come into play. Germany is not France; the Germans are, if not radically, yet sensibly different from the French. Their geographical, political, economic and social features are largely different. But chiefly their historic growth, this, the main factor in a nation's life, differentiates them from the French. The British know much about the French; they know practically nothing about the Germans; whereas the Germans are well acquainted with everything British.

FORMIDABLE BUT BRITTLE

This, then, is the necessary remark that had to be premised in order to give the reader the proper point of view for a right estimation of the strong and weak points of the Germans. With this important proviso, we may now try to study the less advantageous points of the Germans. And in the first place, and before everything else, it must be remarked that the Germans are a power at once formidable and brittle. Powers are measured, not by what they can do when victorious, but by what they are likely to be able to do when misfortune overtakes them.

On consulting history we find that no nation in Europe has proved so brittle, so utterly unable to recover from one fell blow of the fate of battle, as did Prussia, or the dominant State in the German Empire. When in 1806 Napoleon and Davout, on one and the same day, beat the Prussian armies at Jena and Auerstaedt, all Prussia succumbed like a house of cards. Huge, well-garrisoned Prussian fortresses surrendered to a few French cavalry regiments. The collapse of Prussia is unparalleled in all modern history; yet it happened only twenty

years after the death of Prussia's greatest
King, Frederick II., the Great. The men who,
later on, regenerated and rebuilt Prussia, were
all of them non-Prussians. Scharnhorst, Stein,
Blücher were, by birth, no Prussians. Here, in
this fact, is implied one of the greatest failings
of the Prussian system.

That much-imitated system breeds great
measures, but no great men. At any rate, not
a sufficient number of great personalities.
States cannot be made enduringly strong without the possession of the strongest and most
efficient of all assets, that is, Personalities.
There is Frederick II., and Bismarck; but that
is all. The great personalities of the Germans
are literary and artistic, not political, nor military. In denying the Prussians, and the Germans in general, the possession of great military personalities, we seem to expose ourselves
to the sneer of the best-petted prejudices of the
day. Yet we will persist in saying that the
Germans are not likely to have great captains
of war. The German army may be, and no
doubt is, highly organised and disciplined.
But to have a well-trained army is like having
an elaborate dictionary of words. Does the
possession of the dictionary vouchsafe the

possession of a fine style? Style is a matter of personality; so is the style of an army. The greatest nations of all history excelled infinitely less in system and measures, whether political or military, than in the faculty of producing men with a great political or military personality. The Romans, of all nations, had no system whatever.

The Germans, who have written more on Roman history than all other nations put together, have yet never understood the A B C of Roman history. Professor Mommsen, the German "authority" on Roman history, has written up in five big volumes the "system" of the Roman constitution. The truth is, the Romans had no system of their constitution, no more than the modern English have. It was all a matter of personality. Not the edict of the Prætor, but the Prætor himself was the important point.

Just so, in real war, it is not the military ordinances, but the great power of a military personality that wins battles and campaigns. In Germany this is all practically impossible. As great conservatories of music make no really great virtuosi, so the German army system breeds only efficient mediocrities, but no great military personality.   When all goes well, as it did in France in 1870-1871, thanks chiefly to the demoralization of the French, such a Prussian system works admirably.   But when things do not go well, it is bound to come to grief. This can be proved almost mathematically. Since the German system provides not only for normal but also for emergency or problematic cases and since each German officer is bound to obey the given rules to the letter it follows with irrefutable certainty that the German army, in any case of novel situations or of unforeseen yet probable reverses, would be at a loss what to do.   Especially would this be so if the opposing force consisted of officers to whom a broad margin of personal initiative was given.

We are quite aware that much initiative was taken by, if not given to, the German officers in the Franco-German war.   This, however, does not alter matters very much, because that war was, for the Germans, a victorious one from the very start.   It does not indicate what the German officers would do in case of continued reverses; more particularly, if we consider that the Germans have had no great war for now over six-and-thirty years.   Such a long peace is deadly to the rise of free and great military personalities endowed with boundless resourcefulness. We are so strongly convinced of the absolute truth of this statement that we do not hesitate to aver that any great European State that would pass through the practice of a really great war with a European Power other than Germany, would by such a practice alone obtain an immense advantage over the Germans, and eventually beat them. If Austria-Hungary, rousing herself out of her lethargy, would carry on a two years' war with Turkey for the possession of the western part of the Balkans, and if Austria-Hungary came out victorious over the brave and hard-fighting Turks, she would have thereby alone indefinitely increased her chance of beating back a German attack upon her.

The current view that the German army is invincible cannot for a moment be maintained. If an army has gone through a succession of victorious campaigns, and has actually defeated its most important competitors, then, and for the time being, it may be said that such an army is probably invincible. But of an army that has had no great war for more than one generation, it is impossible to say with any degree of certainty whether or no it is invincible. Nobody wants to deny that there is, to use

the words of Napoleon, an art of war, and that
the Germans are doing everything in their
power to carry that art to its highest pitch, as
far as that can be done in times of peace. But
it is equally certain that the art of war, as every
other art, finds its most perfect expression
through a great artist, that is, through a person born to it, and endowed with a great military personality. Now what we here contend is
that the over-systematization and over-regula-
tion of everything connected with the German
army renders the rise of a great German military personality not very probable. Of course,
in the other countries of Europe there is as yet
even less probability of the rise of such a tower-
ing captain. At any rate, we desire to warn
the reader and student of European policy from
assuming too rashly the absolute superiority of
the German army as an engine of war.

The reader may be surprised to hear that in
our opinion the German Navy is very much less
hampered by defects such as we pointed out
with regard to the German Army. In the German Navy there is no secular tradition weigh-
ing upon the elastic members of the service.
The Germans have, in the inhabitants of the
north coast of their empire, a numerous and

hardy sea-faring population. With regard to their chances in maritime warfare they are infinitely less cocksure, hence much less system ridden than with regard to their view of war on land. They do everything to make themselves acquainted with all the physical, geographical and strategic features of the North Sea, and of other seas. At Bergen, in Norway, there is given every year an elaborate course of lectures on everything connected with the nature of the North Sea. The elasticity and greater personal initiative allowed to captains, officers, and crews of German men of war are very remarkable.

PERILS OF BUREAUCRACY

One of the greatest failings of the Germans is their inability to take private and individual initiative in any public affair. Everything is done by the State-paid members of a vast bureaucracy. The State is everything in Germany; Society is, for purposes of public and political life, not in existence at all. As long as there is peace, such a system works admirably. It is a sunny-day system. In times of national reverses the first thing to break down is that very bureaucracy which otherwise forms the prop and mainstay of the people. Once the bureaucracy breaks down, there happens, what we saw in Russia on the breakdown of the Moscovite bureaucracy. Public business cannot be carried on without some men commanding an authority sufficiently great to make people obey them. But where, as in Germany, all authority is monopolised by a bureaucracy, nobody is able to command authority on the break-up of bureaucracy. What saved Rome and has always saved England is the very fact that in both realms there always were men commanding the requisite authority. In Britain such men are, as a rule, not even in office. In Germany they are practically impossible. The constitution of the German Empire was made by Bismarck with the deliberate intention of rendering the rise of politically important but unofficial personalities a practical impossibility.

In case of disaster, unless Germany happens to have an inordinately gifted ruler, she is exposed to greater chances of decomposition than most other nations of Europe. The Germans have never learned the open secret that their greatest achievements in literature, science, philosophy, and music were, as a rule, done by men trammelled by no bonds of officialdom and State-hierarchy. They have never seen, and will never see that what holds good for intellectual greatness, holds good also for greatness political. Instead of having twenty-six rulers as they now have, they would have, had they ever learned the Great Lesson of Politics, twenty-six great and free statesmen; or, in other words, twenty-six possible saviours in times of reverses. Any nation fighting Germany on land must concentrate all its efforts on a considerable initial success, as the surest means of depriving the Germans of most of the advantages now given them by their system.

Germany is in this respect the very contrast to Britain. In the latter country initial successes of the adversary have seldom proved of much importance. The true force of this country came out in times of reverses even much more than in periods of success. In Britain the number of independent men, working on their own initiative and on their own responsibility, is very much greater than that of similar individuals in Germany. Such independent persons have long learned to stand adversity—to be, as the saying is, good losers. This has given to all Britain her peculiar tone, her power in

adversity, her stamina. All this is rather the
exception in Germany. When, in another section of this book, we said that the Germans had
the real spirit of war and imperialism, we always implied that their spirit is the right one
for enterprises promising and giving fair re-
sults. At the present moment we are speaking
of periods of failure, and with regard to such
periods we say that the Germans are considerably less well equipped than are the British.
There is no victory of Zama without the force
to stand the defeat of Cannæ.

Another great drawback for the Germans is
the contemporary international situation regarding a new imperialism. When Spain, Holland, or England started on their careers of
colonising vast and fertile tracts of colonies,
the other Powers in Europe or Asia interfered
with them either not at all, or in a casual manner. Holland, although a tiny country, has still
immense colonies, and used to have very much
more. In those times a few bold captains were
able to lay hold of immense districts in Asia,
Africa, or America. At present this is all well-
nigh impossible. Even in Asia the new and
formidable power of the Japanese has arisen
and would at once veto any violent change in

the distribution of hitherto uncolonised countries. The Colonial and imperial ambitions of the Germans have come in a very unpropitious moment. What formerly could be achieved by a Cortez, Pizarro, Drake, or Frobisher, accompanied by a few gallant fellow adventurers, has now become a vast enterprise, involving hundreds of millions of money and hundreds of thousands of men.

If the reader will carefully contemplate all that the preceding remarks imply, he will arrive at the conclusion that the Germans cannot possibly realise their imperial, and, as we have seen, indispensable ambitions, otherwise than by defeating the Power which both has the most valuable colonies, and is held to command the sea, or the access to such colonies. *Tertium non datur;* a third issue out of the difficulty does not exist. True, one might say that the French would perhaps, in exchange for Alsace and German Lorraine, cede the valuable and large isle of Madagascar to the Germans. Perhaps the French would. But it is certain that no ruler or minister in Germany could seriously think for one moment of proposing the retrocession of Alsace and German Lorraine to the French. He might just as well propose the ces-

sion of Cologne, Frankfort on the Main, or
Berlin.

Just as the Germans made their inner unity
not by persuading one another to unite, as did
the Scots and the English, but by great wars
with Austria, on the one hand, and with France,
on the other; even so they can acquire colonies
not by direct conquest, but only by indirect wars
with England or France. Being the central
country in Europe, the Germans must necessarily use indirect means for their great policy,
whether at home or abroad. For, on account
of their central position, the surrounding
Powers have always so strongly interfered with
the Germans, that the latter could not secure
tranquillity within otherwise than by establishing their superiority abroad. Against this in-
exorable consequence of their central position
there is no other remedy left. We have come
to the strange but nevertheless true conclusion,
that even the weak points of the Germans practically force them to be aggressive. Their undoubted strength prompts them to the same action that their undoubted drawbacks equally en-
tail upon them. Several nations have, in the
course of history, been in a similar position.
It always ended—in one and the same way.

PART III

WE have now reached the end of our task. We have tried to place all the relevant facts of the German Question before the reader. Beginning with a statement of the inordinately over-reaching national vanity of the Germans, we admitted that their international position is one both full of promise and beset with most irritating dangers. While constantly dwelling upon the swelled-head of the Germans, which, unremittingly stimulated by a host of their most popular writers, is constantly growing instead of decreasing, we dwelt with equal insistence on the real power and strength and value of the Germans. None but a malevolent jingo of Berlin can possibly take our work as one deliberately running down or reviling things and persons German.

There is much to be admired in the Germans, and what they have done in the past has laid all the future generations under undying obligations. But here we mainly consider the future.

174

We studied the past in order to foresee the future; just as we always study the present in order to understand more fully the past. In calling attention to German aspirations, to German ambitions, we mean to do a work of honesty, of political honesty. Such among the public men or writers of this country as go on declaring to the people of Great Britain that the Germans harbour no hostile intentions against the British; that, in fact, the relations of the two countries and peoples are the best they can be; such people, we make bold to say, are the enemies of Great Britain. The true friend warns in advance; it is the faddist who, out of sheer conceit, is unable to see the most palpable things, and accordingly does not warn his friend, and so ruins him.

We are quite aware that in this country any enthusiasm or tragic earnestness is discounted with a cold sneer. Nor can we wonder that a nation who, alone of all European nations, remained, for centuries, practically unassailable, has preserved a coolness of nerve which is impossible to Continental nations living under constant menace of ruin. But things have changed. England is no longer unassailable. Europe has now, instead of two fleets, namely the British and the French, as there used to be before, no less than half-a-dozen big fleets, and several minor ones. The whole international, or inter-European, aspect and situation of Great Britain is thoroughly changed. She is, politically, no longer an island.

Only a few years ago many a Briton proudly talked of the "splendid isolation" of Great Britain. Since then that isolation has been deliberately given up, and *entente* is following *entente*. Politically, therefore, we repeat it, England is no longer an island. Nor is she one strategically, or from the standpoint of war. We need not here refer to the series of brilliant and suggestive articles of the Military Correspondent of *The Times* on the perfect feasibleness of an invasion of this country. We simply submit, that a country, whether an island or no, that has no sufficient army of its own, is always exposed to invasion.

Any country, no matter how large, may be compared to a big fortress. Much depends, no doubt, on the strength of the walls and ramparts, bastions and towers. Yet the main force of resistance is in the garrison. Great Britain is the fortress; her navy is the equivalent of the walls and ramparts of that fortress. The national army of England is the garrison of the fortress. The inference from all this is only one: The fortress of Great Britain cannot be declared to be in a state of safety, in that her garrison is far too weak for the purpose. The walls of Great Britain consist practically of about 100,000 seamen. That is far too little for a fortress of the extent of England.

The reader is again reminded that hitherto the great and decisive naval battles of Great Britain have been fought in seas other than the Channel or the North Sea. In the whole of the eighteenth and nineteenth centuries, only two pitched sea-battles were fought by the British in the North Sea; one in 1781, off the Dogger Bank, between Parker and the Dutch Admiral Zouttman, ending in a draw; and the other in 1797, when Duncan, with utmost effort, defeated the Dutch Admiral De Winter. All the great and decisive sea-battles were fought by the British thousands of miles away from England.

The great naval war of the British in the near future will, on the other hand, be fought in the North Sea, and practically there alone. Any decisive advantage of the enemy exposes England at once to an invasion.

Again we say that the Germans have no intention whatever to possess themselves of this country. Such an idea does not enter their minds. This, however, does not exclude a temporary invasion for the purpose of a huge indemnity, or other advantages. Every schoolboy knows that the Dutch Admiral, De Ruyter, entered the Medway in 1667, thanks to strategic advantages which he had secured in the North Sea, and threatened London for some time. The same thing came near happening in 1690, when the French Admiral, Tourville, after defeating the Anglo-Dutch fleet off Beachy Head, made for the entrance of the Thames River. There is no reason to assume that such a thing could not happen again in our time. In war, as in life, everything is possible.

These, then, are the seminal factors of the whole problem: Here is a country, Germany, that having come as the last among the peoples bidding for imperialism and expansion, cannot hope to achieve much by attempts to spread its eagles on the Continent of Europe. It is therefore driven, irremediably driven, to spread by sea-power. Like ancient Carthage, which could not expand into the interior of uninhabitable Africa, Germany too cannot seriously hope to

possess herself of much more territory on the
fully occupied Continent of Europe, and is
forced to spread by maritime power.   However,
Carthage met Rome, that is, a power well-knit
and strongly organised on land, and very capable on sea.   The end was the downfall of Carthage.   Had Rome possessed only sea-power,
Carthage might very well have defeated her.
But Rome had land and sea-power.   Given her
efficient constitution and her twofold power,
Rome could not be worsted in the long run.
Everybody knows that Rome finally defeated
Carthage by means of a land-battle fought on
Carthaginian territory, at Zama.   The Germans, if victorious over the British fleet, can
very well invade England, and hold it for some
time.   The British, with the present organisation of their army, could never think of invad-
ing one town of Germany.   Is such a situation
not threatening enough?   Is it wise to leave
one's enemy a possible advantage so great as
to surpass by far any advantage one may have
over him?

Or, compare the possible losses of the Germans in case of their defeat on sea, with those
of the British in a similar case.   The Germans
would, in the first place, lose all their colonies.

In other words, they would lose what as yet is of little if any value to them. They would furthermore lose heavily in their large Transmarine commerce. The British, on the other hand, would, in case of a naval disaster, lose practically everything. The indemnity which the Germans would exact, would be enormous, both in colonies and in money. Neither Jena nor Sedan could be compared in point of immensity of loss with a decisive naval victory of the Germans over the British fleet. It would be *the* catastrophe of modern times.

Yet in the face of all these facts, there are still thousands and thousands of influential men in this country, who talk of the "impossibility of war with Germany," of the "peaceful and amicable inclinations" of the Germans. Must one really despair to convince the average Briton that wars between civilised nations do *not* depend on the peaceful or amicable inclinations of individuals? Suppose that every German be filled with pure friendship for England. That would not in the least prevent him from going to war with Great Britain. He may love England and the English; yet assuredly he must love his own interest and that of his country very much more intensely. Of passions, the stronger one invariably has the upper hand.

The Germans, as a nation, have never cared for home politics. Their individual indifference and absolute incapacity in that respect have always been so great, that, aided by the disintegrating pressure from outside Powers, they have to the present day not been able to unite into one homogeneous, great and undivided polity. They still are twenty-six different States united into an Empire. Home politics do not interest the German *Bürger,* or burgess. It is quite different with "world-politics," as they call it in the Fatherland. Just because the average German leaves home-politics to the officials and semi-officials, he reserves all his political ardour for "world-politics," or for the hopes and tasks of Imperialism. Nations intensely absorbed in the building up of their home institutions, such as, at present, the Hungarians, or the Italians, do not take much stock in international policy. *Vice versa,* the Germans, having had all their home institutions mapped out for them by their rulers and ministers, concentrate all their fervent interest on the sphere where there still is political activity on a grand scale, offering many a chance of big success to individual ambitionists.

This imperialism, then, is the Great Passion
of the Germans. They are, at present, where
the English were in Elizabethan times. They
burn with the Great Passion. Every one of
them is brimful of it; and no power can stop
or retard that mighty current. The enthusiastic love which every German feels for the
Kaiser is only another way of expressing his
enthusiasm for that vast imperialism which the
Kaiser loves to incarnate in his personality.
Against such a mighty national sentiment, no
mere friendship for other nations can prevail.
Whatever, therefore, individual Germans may
or may not say about the relations of England
and Germany, this cannot in the least alter the
forces driving the latter into antagonism to the
former.

Far more to the point; infinitely more con-
sonant with the dignity, past and future prestige
of Great Britain would it be if all men of leading spirit, all preachers, teachers, statesmen,
journalists, or thinkers of this country joined in
bringing before the nation the necessity of
preparations which, if properly made, would
indeed retard, or eventually frustrate, any attempt on the part of Germany. To talk of universal military service, even if it is done by

Lord Roberts, is hateful to the majority of British citizens. Where the victor in so many battles can carry no conviction, we should be only foolishly presumptuous in trying to convince our readers. The facts of the near future will convince them. Nations are invariably kicked, and never persuaded, into reforms.

Omitting, therefore, any lengthy discussion of this, the one potent means of securing lasting peace between Great Britain and Germany, we only want to point out some evident teachings of history.

The Germans, as we tried to show, are a Power both mighty and brittle. They are brittle, because they do not, and owing to their system, they cannot, have a rich supply of great personalities, whether military or political.

From this it follows with deadly certainty, that a nation that wants to defeat the Germans, must cultivate just the sort of weapon in point of which the Germans are very deficient, that is, mighty, spontaneous personalities. The less the British nation will imitate the manner and method of war obtaining with the Germans, the more she is likely to worst them.

If the Germans, in imitation of the British tendency to big units in sea war, go on building *Dreadnoughts* of an ever-increasing size, the British ought to lay stress on lesser and more nimble units. If the system of the Germans breeds living machines, the British system ought to breed the broadest initiative of captains and officers. If Germany excels in both a strong navy and an exceedingly strong army, Great Britain ought to excel in an exceedingly strong navy and in a strong army. If Germany wants to attack England, England ought to attack her long before.

In the same way, the Bagdad railway, which is practically a German enterprise, ought to be counteracted by a British railway through Beluchistan and Persia. The whole of Great Britain's Asiatic policy ought to be based on the more than fair probability, that Russia does not in the least plan a *coup* on India, as she has never planned it to this day. In the same line of political thought, Great Britain might with great advantage come to an agreement with Holland guaranteeing the contracting parties mutual help for the maintenance of their East-Indian possessions. The commonwealth of Australasia ought to be stimulated into the building of an efficient fleet, so as to be able to

step in with might in any conflict for Great
Britain's Asiatic possessions.

All this and many more measures are dic-
tated by the actual facts of the international
situation of Great Britain and Germany.   For
him who has studied History as a matter of
real life, and not merely as a heap of musty
documents, a description or *précis* of which en-
ables one to get a certificate in an ''exam,'' or
to pose as an ''authority'' in University circles
amongst pedants; for such a man it cannot be
doubtful that, if Great Britain manages her
cards with prudence, she must in the end force
Germany to lower her flag.

Empires are the products of the beginning or
the end of great periods of history.   Antiquity
began and ended with Empires; during its manhood it knew only of intensely developed smaller
States.   Europe is in her manhood; Africa and
Asia are in their infancy.   In Africa and Asia,
therefore, Empires were still possible; but they
have long been made by the British, French,
Russians, Dutch, and a few minor nations, such
as the Belgians or Portuguese.   To win new
Empires in Asia is, since the rise of the mighty
Japanese, quite impossible.   To wrest old ones

from their present possessors is feasible only if
those old possessors persist in making blunder
after blunder.

If, then, we consider the international position
in the light both of history and latter-day politics, we arrive at a conclusion which is indeed a
fearful mortification to the Germans, but nevertheless a sober truth, provided the leading international Powers act according to the elemen-
tary rules of sound politics.

The conclusion is this: On the one hand, the
Germans, for the reasons given all through the
present work, are bound to strive for more expansion, for Imperialism. They do so, they
will do so, with even greater intensity. They
are simply bound to do so. On the other hand,
they cannot possibly establish a really valuable
new Empire, if the old Imperial Powers take
proper measures because they come too late in
the historic day.

Empires are not made where, when, and by
whom it pleases. Had Alexander the Great
been born a hundred years before his actual
date, he could never have defeated the Hellenes,
and therefore, lacking Hellenic help, he could
not have defeated the Persians. Napoleon
would have done nothing without the French

Revolution. It was that extraordinary event that gave birth to extraordinary military talents, which in turn helped Napoleon to win the battles of Rivoli, Marengo, Austerlitz, and Jena. The Germans want to make a vast Empire with the help of a strict system, and out of sheer intention and resolution, without any help from a great historic event in their favour.

Had the British lost South Africa in the late Boer War, which, as Col. F. N. Maude himself has pointed out, was far from an impossibility in the first six weeks of the war (see *The Times Literary Supplement* of May 31, 1907), then indeed the loss of British prestige would have constituted, for Germany, one of those historic events that enable other Powers to step in and achieve new imperial triumphs. But given that new Empires are, for the present, unhistoric, not to say unnatural; given that the Germans, however so badly they need such an Empire, ought not to be able to acquire it, so long as Great Britain follows the clear dictates of her past and her present; there remains nothing for the Germans but to give up the dream of Pan-Germanism.

Should Great Britain, misled by men who have never made a serious study of either history or of the Continent in its present configuration, misread the signs of the time, and instead of meeting the inevitable aggressiveness of the Germans by due preparations, continue to treat the German Question lightly, or ignore it altogether, then indeed the dream of Pan-Germanism will not remain a dream.

By a similar misreading of Continental politics, England lost in the eighteenth century her vast American colonies. Of course, the average Briton is not at all aware of this broad historic fact. He thinks that the Yankees "wrested" their country from the British. Nothing is less true. The loss of the present United States was caused, as we have shown in a separate work, almost exclusively by the foolishly provoked hostility of France, Holland, and Spain against Great Britain. The British fleet was worsted by the French fleet, both in America and in India, and consequently the American colonies were lost.

Should the signs of the time again be misread, then there is no reason for the Germans to despair of the success of their vast ambitions. They bide their time; they want to wait for a moment when Great Britain will commit blunders similar to those that caused the loss of the present United States, a loss greater than any Empire ever sustained. Such blunders of their adversary are in reality the foundation of their policy. They began the war with France because they positively knew that France was not properly prepared. They mean to do the same thing with Great Britain.

It is in the hopes of rousing the British nation to this danger, that the present little book is written. The Germans, the author holds, must expand, will expand, but ought not to be able to establish a new Empire at the expense of the British Empire, as long as Great Britain, fully cognisant of the imminent danger of Germany's Swelled Head, prepares for the conflict both from the military and naval standpoint, let alone by means of judicious diplomacy. Late comers must be satisfied with crumbs; if they get more, it is only because there is something radically wrong with the people who preceded them.

EPILOGUE

THAT Dr. Reich's conception of the Kaiser's objects and the temper of the German people was substantially correct has been proved beyond the shadow of a doubt. The Kaiser has fired the mine which he laid, and his action has been applauded by the majority of his subjects. We propose to supplement the evidence collected by Dr. Reich. His book was written under the impression made by the Kaiser's violent attitude towards France on the question of Morocco. Let us observe the diplomatic activities of William II., both before and after that date. Never in the history of the world has there been a more striking exhibition of insane wickedness and cunning than the German Emperor's.

AN IMPERIAL MACHIAVELLI

The machinations of German diplomacy lay at the back of the trouble in the Far East which culminated in the Russo-Japanese War. William II. had proclaimed that the Yellow Races were a peril to European civilisation, and he had embodied the idea in a poorly executed picture presented to the Czar. After the Chinese-Japanese War, Germany, with Russia and France, deprived the Japanese of Port Arthur. Two years later (1897) the Germans began the dismemberment of China by seizing Kiao-Chau, and, immediately afterwards, Port Arthur was occupied by Russia. The occupation of Port Arthur by the Russians was bound, sooner or later, to cause hostilities between the Czar and the Mikado, and the astute soldiers at Berlin could have had little doubt in their own minds as to the result of a struggle between the highly efficient and patriotic Japanese Army and Navy and the Russian land and marine forces in the Far East.

By encouraging the Czar to embark on the Russo-Japanese War—the Russians received an assurance that they would not be attacked by Germany during the continuance of the Manchurian campaign—the Kaiser and his ministers were an efficient cause of the War, and of the subsequent risings in Russia. When the Kaiser visited Tangier on March 31, 1905, and interfered in the settlement of Morocco, the Russian armies were retiring before Japanese troops trained by Germans. The sinister policy of

Germany towards Russia had been successful.

A similar policy had been pursued by Germany towards the British Empire. The Boers had been encouraged to believe that they could count on German support if they endeavoured to subjugate the British in South Africa. It will be remembered that in the Eighties of the last century, Krüger had been entertained at Berlin by Bismarck, and it must have been with the deliberate intention of deceiving the Boers and hastening a South African War that the Kaiser despatched his telegram to the Boer President. "I sincerely congratulate you," the imperial Machiavelli cabled, "that, without making any appeal for the help of foreign Powers, you have succeeded, with your people and your own strength, in repulsing the armed bands which have troubled the peace of your land."

The Kaiser had, however, not the slightest wish to assist the Russians against the Japanese, or the Boers against the English. At the interview, a report of which was published by the *Daily Telegraph* on October 28, 1908, he even claimed to have prevented Russia and France from attacking us during the Boer War, and to have sketched out the plan of campaign executed by Lords Roberts and Kitchener!

Assuming—it is a large assumption—that these statements are true, we are not in his debt. Prince Von Bülow, his Ex-Chancellor, has kindly explained his master's motives. "Among the French," says the Prince, "the deeply rooted national hatred against the Germans would speedily and completely have ousted the momentary ill-feeling against England as soon as we had definitely committed ourselves to a course hostile to her [Great Britain's] interests. . . . During those years we were occupied in founding our sea power by building the German navy, and, even in the event of [British] defeat in the South African War, it was possible to stifle our sea power in the embryo." [1]

Thus, without the loss of a Pomeranian grenadier, the Kaiser's iniquitous diplomacy had crippled Russia, endangered the French savings invested in Russia, saddled Great Britain with an enormous debt, and sacrificed the lives and fortunes of innumerable Russians, Japanese, Britons, and Boers.

[1] *Imperial Germany*, by Prince Von Bülow, translated by Marie A. Lewenz, M.A. (Dodd, Mead & Co.), pp. 31-2.

A BID FOR MAHOMETAN SUPPORT

Another blow aimed at the British Empire may yet be successful and lead to the massacre of all Europeans (including Germans) isolated among Mahometans.

Two years after cabling to Krüger—in 1898—William II. paid a visit to the Sultan of Turkey, Abdul Hamid, who had been extirpating the Armenians. From Damascus he thanked that miscreant for his hospitality. "May the Sultan," he said, "and the three hundred million Mussulmans scattered over the earth be assured that the German Emperor will always be their friend." [2]   Since 1883 the Turkish Army—once trained by Moltke—had been reorganised by the celebrated German strategist, Von der Goltz. As the majority of Mussulmans live in the British Empire, and large numbers of them in French colonies, the Kaiser's object in courting the Mussulmans was obvious. His theatrical pilgrimage to the Holy Land in 1898 gave him an opportunity of inspecting the country through which a German-

---

[2] *Germany and the German Emperor,* by George H. Perris (Melrose), p. 410; *Imperial Germany,* by Prince Von Bülow, p. 84.

Turkish Army would march on the Suez Canal
and Egypt, while the Bagdad Railway, permis-
sion for the construction of which was secured
by German financiers in 1899, was probably designed to enable him to throw troops into India
where he doubtless hoped to find support from
the Mahometans and Bengalese.

The Bagdad Railway is a continuation of the
German Anatolian Railway, which had been
constructed earlier. Russia, defeated and in
the throes of a Revolution, it was expected,
would not be able to prevent Germany, Austria-
Hungary and Turkey, between them, from
coercing the Balkan States, and, but for the for-
tunate defeat of the Turkish Army and the re-
vival of Russia, German troops might to-day be
on the shores of the Persian Gulf and in Egypt.
Writing in October, 1911, General Von Bernhardi observed that "Turkey—the predominant
Power of the Near East—is of paramount importance to us [the Germans]. She is our natural ally. . . . Turkey is . . . the only Power
which can threaten England's position in
Egypt, and thus menace the short sea-route and
the land communications to India." [3]

[3] *Germany and the Next War*, by General Friedrich von Bernhardi, translated by Allen H. Powles (Edward Arnold), p. 99.

The short sea-route to India would be threatened by Turkey; the next step was to obtain a position from which Germany could command our long sea-route. If she could obtain ports on the coast of Morocco she might cut both arteries. The people of Morocco, also, are Mahometans. Consequently, in 1905, the Kaiser suddenly assumed the rôle of protector of Morocco while Russia, France's ally, was embarrassed by the war with Japan. If his fleet had been powerful enough, he would presumably have followed up his intervention by overt acts of hostility. As it was, he had to be content with driving M. Delcassé from the French Foreign Office, and procuring the Algeciras Conference.

The Russian Baltic fleet was destroyed by the Japanese at the Battle of Tsu-Shima (May 27-28, 1905); on June 6, M. Delcassé resigned, and, on the same day, Count Von Bülow was created a Prince. It was *after,* not *before* Sedan that Bismarck had been promoted to the same rank. The services for which Von Bülow was rewarded may be surmised. From the standpoint of a disciple of Machiavelli, Frederick the Great, Napoleon, and Bismarck, the policy towards Russia, the British Empire, and France had been masterly.

RUSSIA FLOUTED

So far, the Kaiser, judged by Atheist and
Anti-Social standards, had been very successful. At the Algeciras Conference (1906), no
doubt, he discovered that the United States and
Italy, the third member of the Triple Alliance,
were not prepared to promote German ambitions. Nevertheless he had triumphantly asserted Germany's right to be consulted in the
Morocco settlement, and he had been supported
by Austria-Hungary. "You showed yourself,"
said the Kaiser, addressing his ally, "a brilliant
second in the tourney, and can reckon on the like
service from me on a similar occasion."

This occasion was not long in coming. In
1907, at the Guildhall, William II. assured the
British Public that his aim was above all "the
preservation of peace." But in 1908, at his
instigation or with his connivance, Austria-
Hungary annexed Bosnia-Herzegovina, two
Turkish provinces held by her in trust under the
Berlin Treaty. It was at the suggestion of the
late Marquess of Salisbury that Austria-Hungary had received a mandate to administer this
territory.

The annexation was, of course, a challenge to

Servia and Russia. The Kaiser, by threats,
obliged Russia to swallow the insult. To use
his own histrionic phrase, he "took his stand in
shining armour" by the side of the Emperor
Francis Joseph.

It was a few days after the annexation of
Bosnia-Herzegovina (October 7, 1908) that the
interview with him, already referred to, appeared in the *Daily Telegraph* (October 28,
1908). In this interview he alleged that one of
his dearest wishes "was to live on the best
terms with England, though the prevailing sentiment among large portions of the middle"
(why not the upper?) "and lower classes of his
own people was not friendly to England." On
February 17 of the same year he had written
privately to Lord Tweedmouth, then First Lord
of the Admiralty, with a view to influencing our
naval programme. "Lord Esher," he is reported to have written, "had better attend to
the drains at Windsor and leave alone matters
which he does not understand." Lord Esher
had not accepted the Kaiser's promises at their
face value.

Not unnaturally, the interview in the *Daily
Telegraph* aroused a storm of indignation
among the Germans. The manuscript, it was

explained to them, had been sent by the Emperor to the Chancellor who alleged that he had not read it. Probably to deceive the peace-lovers in England and elsewhere, the Kaiser was publicly reproved by Prince Von Bülow. It was to the advantage of the plotters in Berlin to make us believe that the German had become a fettered despotism.

THE COUP D'AGADIR

Having humiliated Russia, the Kaiser again attempted to humiliate France. In July, 1911, the *Panther* was despatched to Agadir and the Algeciras settlement of the Morocco question reopened. To escape from war, France was obliged to surrender—it is true in return for the Protectorate of Morocco—a large part of her territory on the Congo, and, but for the (to the Germans) unexpected firmness of the British Government, it is probable that Germany would have acquired a naval base in Morocco, menacing our Mediterranean and West African trade routes. The arrangement with France after the *coup d'Agadir* will, perhaps, be marked as the last triumph of German diplomacy.

BALKAN TROUBLE AND GERMAN POLICY

The Kaiser's murderous friend, the Sultan Abdul, had been deposed by the Young Turks in 1909, but German officers were still drilling the Turkish army, and its armaments were being made in Germany. After the Agadir incident, Italy declared war on Turkey—"in direct opposition," says General Von Bernhardi, "to the interests of the Triple Alliance"—and conquered Tripoli. "This undertaking," pursues the General, "brought her to the brink of a war with Austria, which, *as the supreme Power in the Balkan Peninsula,* can never tolerate the encroachment of Italy into those regions." [4] The next year (1912) the Turkish Army, despite its German training and German weapons, was decisively defeated in nearly every encounter with the Bulgarians, Servians, Greeks and Montenegrins. The Turks failed to exhibit "the high military qualities" [5] with which Von Bernhardi had credited them. Had it not been for the folly of the Bulgarians in quarrelling with the Servians and Greeks, the German aims, so far as the Balkans were concerned, might have had

[4] *Germany and the Next War,* p. 86: the italics are ours.
[5] Ibid., p. 141.

to be postponed indefinitely. There is strong ground for suspicion that Bulgaria, ruled by a German prince, was thrust on Servia by the Germans and Austrians.

The second of the Balkan wars (though it ended in the triumph of Servia, Greece and Roumania), by further exhausting Servia, encouraged Germany and Austria-Hungary to pursue their aggressive policy. There can now be no manner of doubt that last year Germany was preparing to shake "the mailed fist" at Russia and her Allies. The Kaiser, in 1913, raised a huge war-benevolence from his subjects, a considerable part of which, it may be noted, was allocated to the air-fleet.

THE GERMANS VERSUS THE WORLD

We come now to the diplomatic intercourse immediately antecedent to the present war. Was war deliberately planned for 1914? It is open to doubt. "Let it be the task of our diplomacy," General Von Bernhardi adjured his superiors, "so to shuffle the cards that we may be attacked by France, for then there would be reasonable prospect that Russia for a time would remain neutral."[6] He remarked else-

[6] *Germany and the Next War*, p. 290.

where (p. 296) that the Agadir Convention was "as liable to revision as the Algeciras treaty, and, indeed, offers, in this respect, the advantage that it creates new opportunities of friction with France." According to him, "the German Government, from important reasons which could not be discussed," had in 1911 "considered it expedient to avoid, under present conditions, a collision with England or France at any cost" (p. 294). It is significant that our Ambassador at St. Petersburg telegraphed on the 30th July last, to Sir Edward Grey, that the "German ambassador had a second interview with Minister for Foreign Affairs at 2 a.m., when former *completely broke down on seeing that war was inevitable*. He appealed to M. Sazonof," added Sir G. Buchanan, "to make some suggestion which he could telegraph to German Government as a last hope." [7]

We learn also from another despatch that, in the opinion of the Russian Minister for Foreign Affairs, "Germany was unfortunate in her representatives in Vienna and St. Petersburg; the former was a violent Russophobe, who had urged Austria on, the latter had reported to his

[7] *Correspondence respecting the European Crisis* (*Parliamentary White Paper No. 6, 1914, Price 9d.*), p. 53.

Government that Russia would never go to war."[8]

The domestic difficulties of Great Britain, France and Russia, however, decided the tiger at Berlin to spring.

The arming of Ulster and the Nationalists, the refusal of the army officers in Ireland to execute the British Cabinet's orders, the resignation of their posts by Sir John French and other eminent officers, the undoubted strength of the Socialists and Syndicalists in Great Britain and the apparent strength of the Peace-at-any-price Party among us seemed to afford to the materialists at Potsdam a reasonable hope that we might accept their "infamous proposal" to remain neutral while Belgium and France were being crushed and despoiled of their colonies.

Moreover, if Von Bernhardi's book reflects the workings of the military brains of the Prussian and Austro-Hungarian Armies, the British fleet has alone been taken into account by the German strategists. Our Colonial militia, he remarks (p. 137), "can be completely ignored so far as concerns any European theatre of war," and "it is very questionable whether the English army is capable of effectively acting

[8] Ibid., p. 71.

on the offensive against Continental European
troops" (p. 151). Though he does not criticise
the Belgian Army, we surmise, from his observation that Holland "would easily yield to
a German invasion" (p. 144), that no resistance
was anticipated—by him at all events—from
Belgium.

France, also, to superficial observers, appeared this year to be drifting towards a Revolution. The murder of M. Calmette and the
croakings of an unpatriotic Senator as to the
unpreparedness of the Army may have led the
Germans astray. As for Russia: it may well
have been believed that she had not recovered
from her war with Japan and from the Revolution which was still smouldering.

To personages like the Kaiser and the Crown
Prince the political situation appeared too
tempting. The German Crown Prince, if
gauged by his utterances, loves bloodshed and
brutality, and the Kaiser gives the impression
that he firmly believes himself to be a super-
Napoleon. "I cannot stand him any longer,"
said the grim realist, Bismarck, " . . . I cannot make genuflexions, or crouch under the table
like a dog. He wants to break with Russia.
. . . I cannot tack on as a tail to my career the

failures of arbitrary and inexperienced self-conceit for which I should be held responsible.''

The Kaiser's self-conceit is the primary cause of the war; and, as Mr. F. W. Wile in his article in the *Daily Mail* of the 14th of August points out, the treacherous inspection of our armament firms made by the head of the firm of Krupp and his expert between June 14 and 23—i.e. *before the murder of the heir to the throne of Austria-Hungary*—must have been inspired by the Kaiser.

"Although I am not able to verify it," telegraphed our ambassador at Vienna to Sir Edward Grey on the 30th of July, "I have private information that the German ambassador knew the text of the Austrian ultimatum to Servia before it was despatched, and telegraphed it to the German Emperor." [9] The following passage from a telegram sent by Sir H. Rumbold from Berlin to Sir Edward Grey is also worth noting, "Emperor returns suddenly to-night, and Under-Secretary of State for Foreign Affairs says that Foreign Office regret this step, which was taken on His Majesty's own initiative." [10]

[9] *Correspondence respecting the European Crisis*, p. 52.
[10] Ibid., p. 21.

Admiral Mahan pronounces that the Kaiser's absence from Berlin at the opening of the crisis was a mere ruse of war. After the "infamous proposal" made to Great and Greater Britain, it is impossible to give William II. the benefit of the doubt.

THE ETHICS AND OPINIONS OF WILLIAM II.

The Kaiser has provoked millions of men to kill millions of other men. Owing to him, innumerable women and children will be murdered or die of starvation, and the products of the labour of countless human beings destroyed or wasted. Already some of his subjects have discovered this. The committee of the German Humanity League, Berlin, have sent to the British Humanity League a document in which he is characterised as "the uncurbed tyrant, surrounded by parasites, now directing the most desperate, devilish, and selfish campaign ever waged against humanity"; as "the despot whose insatiable egotism is drenching Europe with the blood of its workers and wage-earners" (*Times*, Aug. 15, 1914).

The Prussian statesman Stein called Napoleon "the great criminal," but Napoleon had this excuse, that he issued from the French

Revolution, that he was a man of vast ability and that, in the existing condition of things, his reforms—and he made many and useful reforms—had to be forced on mankind at the point of the bayonet. One wonders what epithet Stein or, say, Kant would have applied to William II. and his councillors! That the Kaiser's ethics are peculiar may be gathered from his address to the German soldiers despatched to China in 1900.

As reported by the Bremen *Weser Zeitung* he said:—

"When you meet the foe you will defeat him. No quarter will be given, no prisoners will be taken. Let all who fall into your hands be at your mercy...Just as the Huns a thousand years ago, under the leadership of Etzel (Attila) gained a reputation in virtue of which they still live in historical tradition, so may the name of Germany become known in such a manner in China that no Chinaman will ever again even dare to look askance at a German." (*Times*, July 30, 1900, p. 5.)

The reference to Attila was commonly suppressed, but the rest of the quotation was circulated on postcards throughout Germany. (*Times*, Aug. 11, 1900, p. 4.)

Two days later, the modern Attila preached a sermon on board the *Hohenzollern*.

"We will mobilise," he is reported by the *Kreuz Zeitung* to have said, "not only battalions of warriors, but also a holy force of supplicants. And there is much that we have to beg and pray for on behalf of our brethren who are going forth to fight. They are to be the strong arm that is to chastise the assassins. They are to be the mailed fist that is to strike into the midst of these wild deeds." (*Times,* Aug. 3, 1900, p. 4.)

The Kaiser is not more tender to his own subjects than to the Chinese. "It may happen, though God forbid," he told some recruits at Potsdam on November 23, 1891, "that *you may have to fire on your own parents or brothers. Prove your fidelity then by your sacrifice.*" [11] Whether he believes in a God is a moot point. On another occasion he said to some soldiers, "You must all have only one will, and it is mine; there is only one law, and it is mine." [12]

Of the nauseating doses of flattery which the Emperor has administered to his subjects here are a few samples :—

[11] *Germany and the German Emperor, sup. cit.,* p. 391.
[12] Ibid., p. 390.

(1) "The German people are the salt of the earth."

(2) "To us Germans great ideals have become permanent possessions, whereas to other peoples they have been, more or less, lost."

(3) "Far stretches our speech over the ocean, far the flight of our science and exploration; no work in the domain of new discovery, no scientific idea but is first tested by us and then adopted by other nations. This is the world-rule the German spirit strives for."

(4) "Our German people will be the granite block on which the good God may complete His work of civilising the world. Then will be realised the word of the poet who said that the world will one day be cured by the German character."

(5) "Berlinese sculpture has reached a degree of perfection that the Renaissance would scarcely surpass."

THE INFLUENCE OF BISMARCK

One would need the pen of Voltaire to portray the Kaiser. His sole excuses are that when a boy he came under the influence of the cynical Bismarck, and that his conceptions of Germany and War are shared by a large number of semi-civilised Germans. Let Bismarck himself describe how he tampered with the Ems telegram and produced the Franco-German War.

"Having decided to resign" (the grandfather of the Kaiser was, comparatively speaking, a humane man and wished, if possible, to avoid a war with France, and Bismarck wanted to resign if there was no war) "in spite of the remonstrances which Roon made against it, I invited him and Moltke to dine with me alone. . . . During our conversation I was informed that a telegram from Ems . . . was being deciphered. When the copy was handed to me it showed that Abeken had drawn up and signed the telegram at His Majesty's command, and I read it out to my guests, *whose dejection was so great that they turned away from food and drink.* . . . I put a few questions to Moltke as to the extent of our preparations. . . . He answered that if there was to be war he expected no advantage to us by deferring the outbreak. . . . I made use of the royal authorisation communicated to me through Abeken, to publish the contents of the telegram, and, in the presence of my two guests, I reduced the telegram by striking out words, but without adding or altering. . . . After I had read out the concentrated edition . . . Moltke remarked: 'Now it has a different ring: it sounded before like a parley; now it is like a flourish in answer to a challenge.' I went on to explain: 'If I at once communicate the text . . . not only to the newspapers, but also by telegraph to all our Embassies, it will be known in Paris before midnight, and . . . will have the effect of a red rag upon the Gallic bull.'' [13]

Bismarck had a patriotic reason for his conduct in sub-editing the telegram—Napoleon III, and Francis Joseph were undoubtedly preparing to attack Prussia—but it was an abominable action on his part to reveal later the fraudulent method by which he provoked the war. By doing so he destroyed any moral justification the Germans had for retaining Alsace-Lorraine, and he poisoned the minds of the present generation of Germans. And he did it merely to gratify his hatred for the Kaiser! If one of the foremost of Prussian patriots behaved in this cynical and selfish way, what can the world expect from the average Prussian officer and bureaucrat?

[13] *Bismarck, his Reflections and Reminiscences*, translated under the supervision of A. J. Butler, late Fellow of Trinity College, Cambridge, pp. 95–100.

Englishmen will have read with pitying amusement the vapourings of the Anglo-German Houston Chamberlain (see pp. 11-14, 37-39). It may interest them to know that his theories are merely a development of some table-talk of Bismarck reported by his jackal, Busch. "The Germans," said the Man of Blood and Iron, "the Germanic race is, so to speak, the male principle throughout Europe—the fructifying principle. The Celtic and Slav peoples represent the female sex. . . . The Revolution of 1789 was the overthrow of the German element by the Celtic." [14]

PRUSSIAN ATHEISM

Bismarck was primarily a civilian. Views akin to those held by him appear in magnified forms in the writings of German soldiers. Below are the reflections of the late Count Yorck von Wartenburg, Colonel of the General Staff of the Prussian Army, on Napoleon's horrible order to his Adjutant-General "to convey all the gunners and other Turks who were captured at Jaffa with arms in their hands to the seashore, and have them shot, taking care that

[14] *Bismarck, Some Secret Pages of His History,* by Busch, I. 526–7.

none escape,"—an order rightly denounced by every Christian historian.

"In the eyes of mere didactic historical writers," said Count Von Wartenburg, "this deed may appear horrible and revolting, but practical military history must not consider it as such. . . . If such an act is necessary for the safety of one's army, it is not only justified, but its repetition in any future war will be advisable, and no convention could alter this fact."

Comment on such comments is superfluous. As Mr. Belloc remarks, "Prussia is . . . Atheist. Her Atheism has profoundly penetrated the private morals of her people. It has not only penetrated, it has permeated the mind of her rulers."

Again: the ex-trainer of the Turks, Field-Marshal Von der Goltz, assures us that "wars are the fate of mankind, the inevitable destiny of nations," and that "inexorability and seemingly hideous callousness are among the attributes necessary to him who would achieve great things in war. In the case of the general there is only one crime for which history never pardons him, and that is—defeat." [15]

[15] *The Nation in Arms*, by Baron Colmar Von der Goltz, translated by Philip A. Ashworth (pp. 470 and 79).

One of the greatest American generals in the North and South War said that war was "Hell," and Napoleon himself, if Ségur is to be trusted, considered it to be "a game of barbarians," the art of which consisted in being stronger than the enemy at a given point. The language of Von der Goltz, Von Wartenburg and the Kaiser takes one back to the days of the Thirty Years' War, of Timour, of Attila or of the Assyrians.

GERMANS AND MILITARISM

The writer of these lines was a few days ago in Switzerland, living on the most friendly terms with several Germans, among them two frank and kind-hearted youths who spent much of their time amusing some French children. Both of these lads were suddenly summoned to join, one the German Fleet, the other the German Army. Among the writer's friends has been a German of vast intelligence, extraordinary modesty, and unaffected kindliness. How many among us have had similar experiences! That a well-educated people, hospitable and fond of family life, should be used as his jemmy by the strange intelligence who has pronounced Count Zeppelin to be "the greatest man of the century'' is a tragedy unequalled in the world's history.

The monsters who have made this War have taken the fullest advantage of the enormous and portentous superiority possessed to-day by the armed over the unarmed man, and also of the facilities afforded by the printing-press to stimulate the vanity, fears, and hatreds of human beings. The barbarous behaviour of the Prussian officers in Alsace-Lorraine and now in Belgium, the tales of horror which, from time to time, have reached us from the German Colonies, show the nature of the tyranny which the Prussian camarilla is seeking to impose on the white and coloured races. If Prussia were to succeed, it is probable that the institution of slavery would be revived. The friends of the Turks and condoners of the Armenian massacres would have no compunction in coercing men to satisfy their needs and unnatural caprices. "England," observes General Von Bernhardi, "committed the unpardonable blunder, from her point of view, of not supporting the Southern States in the American War of Secession." [16] That the Southern States wished to preserve and extend their

[16] *Germany and the Next War*, p. 92.

"domestic institution" of slavery ought not, of course, to have deterred us!

At the trial of Dr. Peters, the High Commissioner for German East Africa, who, *inter alia,* had flogged and executed a woman, the Disciplinary Court at Berlin observed: "With regard to the flogging of the women, it may be admitted that flogging is a customary punishment for women as well as for men in Africa." General Von Liebert, ex-Governor of the province, gave evidence and remarked that "in Africa it is impossible to get on without cruelty," and that the condemnation of Dr. Peters (he lost his post) was "a stain and disgrace upon German justice and the German people." [17] This general was a member of the Reichstag and President of the Anti-Socialist League.

Rightly regarded, the war against Germany is a war for the liberation of the German nation, and the sooner that we make that clear to them the better. In the Napoleonic War, the Allies declared that they were waging war on Napoleon alone, and in the Franco-German War the Prussian rulers—but falsely—alleged that their enemy was Napoleon III. and not the French

[17] *The Times,* July 1, 1907.

people. The mass of the Germans, it cannot be too often repeated, have been grossly deceived by their Government, and by most of their Professors and Publicists. If any one doubts this, let him procure General Von Bernhardi's classic; a cheap edition of the translation has been issued by Mr. Edward Arnold. From that amazingly candid work we append some extracts.

(1) "The German people" is "the greatest civilised people known to history" (p. 6).

If so, their behaviour is curious. "Gentlemen," said the German Chancellor on August 4 to the Reichstag, "we are now in a state of necessity, and necessity knows no law! Our troops have occupied Luxemburg, and perhaps are already on Belgian soil. Gentlemen, that is contrary to the dictates of international law. . . . The wrong—I speak openly—that we are committing we will endeavour to make good as soon as our military goal has been reached. Anybody who is threatened, as we are threatened, and is fighting for his highest possessions, can have only one thought—how he is to hack his way through."

Germany was supporting Austria-Hungary and Austria-Hungary had sent to Servia an ultimatum the like of which has never been delivered since the Age of Napoleon. Sir Edward Grey, who is not accustomed to exaggerate, told Count Mensdorff that he had "never before seen one State address to another independent State a document of so formidable a character." That the real author of the ultimatum was the clement prince who ordered his soldiers to give no quarter to Chinamen is not improbable. Servia, moreover, had practically accepted the terms of the ultimatum. To murder, to beggar, and to burn the houses of neutrals is a natural action on the part of "the greatest civilised people known to history."

(2) "From the time of their first appearance in history, the Germans showed themselves a firstclass civilised people" (p. 53).

The Romans and Greeks who first came in contact with them would not have agreed with the General. The Goths and the Vandals were Germans.

(3) "The proud conviction forces itself upon us with irresistible power that a high,

if not the highest, importance for the entire development of the human race is ascribable to this German people" (p. 68).

General Von Bernhardi is more modest than his master (see p. 163).

(4) "Two great movements were born from the German intellectual life, on which, henceforth, *all* the intellectual and moral progress of man *must* rest: the Reformation and the critical philosophy" (p. 69).

The italics are ours. General Von Bernhardi is trespassing on the Kaiser's province! The Chinese had the impertinence to invent gunpowder and printing. *Gothic* architecture came from France. The Renaissance commenced in Italy; Italians discovered America, a Pole, Copernicus, the heliocentric system; and Shakespeare, Bacon, Newton and Watt had the misfortune to be Englishmen, Fulton to be an American. Wycliffe, too, was born before Luther, and Hus happened to be a Bohemian. The Emperor Sigismund who sent Hus to the stake was, however, a German.

(5) "From the point of view of civilisation, it is imperative to preserve the Ger-

man spirit, and by so doing to establish foci of universal culture'' (p. 75).

Cannot "foci of universal culture" be established without the assistance of Krupp and his agents? One would suppose that a Chinese Wall had been erected round Germany! That German culture is synonymous with "universal culture" is a hard saying. Their printed alphabet and their language, to take two examples, are very clumsy vehicles for the transmission of thought. It may surprise the *soldat de plume,* as Napoleon would have called him, to learn that there have been scientists, artists, and men of letters, who were not, or are not Germans. Faraday and Darwin were Englishmen, Pasteur and Balzac were Frenchmen, Metchnikoff is and Tolstoi was Russian, Chopin was a Pole, Edison is an American, Marconi is an Italian. The Germans have devoted themselves to the study of Antiquity, but the most brilliant and penetrating study of the Ancient World has been written by an Italian, Ferrero, who, however, had the bad taste—long before Mr. Norman Angell—to expose the folly and wickedness of the German conception of War. Of course, no one denies that the world is heavily indebted to the race which has produced Leibnitz, Bach, Lessing, Kant, Niebuhr, Savigny, Goethe, Schiller, Beethoven, Gauss, Virchow, Wagner, Köch, and Ehrlich.

(6) "No people is so little qualified as the German to direct its own destinies" (p. 112). On this point General Von Bernhardi enlarges.

(a) Germany is "a country . . . torn asunder internally and externally" (p. 128).

(b) The Germans "have to-day become a peace-loving—an almost 'too' peace-loving—nation" (p. 2).

(c) The German character is "good-natured" (p. 2).

(d) The Germans "wish not to be disturbed in commercial life" (p. 2).

It is strange that this, "the greatest civilised people known to history," is "so little qualified to direct its own destinies." It is not so strange that the Germans "wish not to be disturbed in commercial life."

(7) "When the State renounces all extension of power, and recoils from every

> war which is necessary for its expansion
> . . . then its citizens become stunted. . . .
> This is sufficiently exemplified by the pitia-
> ble existence of all small States'' (p. 19).

And the City States of Athens and Florence
produced a finer art and literature than the
vast German and Roman Empires!

Von Bernhardi, general and statesman, is
more illuminating than Von Bernhardi, historian and sociologist. There is no need to
comment on the following quotations.

(1) "Nothing is left but war to secure to
the true elements of progress the ascendency over the spirits of corruption and de-
cay'' (p. 13).

(2) War is "a moral obligation, and, as
such, an indispensable factor in civilisation'' (p. 17).

(3) "From the Christian standpoint we
arrive at the same conclusion'' (p. 22).

(4) "The efforts directed towards the
abolition of war must not only be termed
foolish, but absolutely immoral, and must
be stigmatised as unworthy of the human
race'' (p. 27).

(5) "France must be so completely

crushed that she can never again come across our path" (p. 104).

(6) "The principle of the balance of power in Europe . . . must be entirely disregarded" (p. 107).

(7) "A pacific agreement with England is, after all, a will-o'-the-wisp which no serious German statesman would trouble to follow" (p. 97).

(8) "Our next war will be fought for the highest interests of our country and of mankind. This will invest it with importance in the world's history. 'World power or downfall!' will be our rallying cry" (p. 156).

IN CONCLUSION

So long as the German nation was under the control of armed men like the Kaiser, his son, and General Von Bernhardi, a war between the German and the British Empires could scarcely have been prevented.

When estimating the chances of Germany and Austria-Hungary, the Omnisciences at Berlin seem to have left one or two important factors out of their calculations. The Russian Army has been through the furnace of the Russo-

Japanese War; the Servians distinguished themselves in the two Balkan Wars; the French have had numerous opportunities of discovering, under war conditions, the nature of modern warfare, while the British Army was tested by the Boers. The German and Austro-Hungarian soldiers, on the other hand, are amateurs, very few of them having been in action.

At the risk of seeming irrelevance, we shall close by quoting an appreciation of Lord Kitchener made by a Prussian Staff Officer, Major Von Tiedmann, who, as military attaché, accompanied the British army in the Soudan campaign. "Lord Kitchener," he wrote, "was familiar with the country and people of the Soudan and all facts concerned with it; he spoke Arabic well, and it would have been difficult to find a more suitable person for the conduct of the campaign. . . . He waited unconcernedly for the right moment; but, when it came, he pounced with eagle-like swiftness and sureness upon his prey, and dealt the decisive blow in a surprisingly short time. He had neglected nothing."

J. B. R.